£7.95.
c.

FAMILY
WORK
IN
ACTION

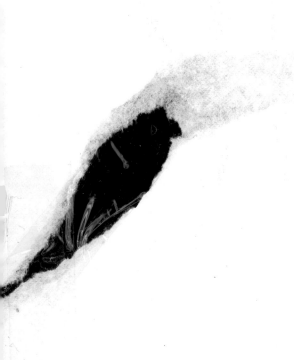

FAMILY
WORK
IN
ACTION

A HANDBOOK
FOR SOCIAL WORKERS

EDITED BY
ODED MANOR

TAVISTOCK PUBLICATIONS
LONDON AND NEW YORK

First published in 1984 by
Tavistock Publications Ltd
11 New Fetter Lane,
London EC4P 4EE

Published in the USA by
Tavistock Publications
in association with Methuen, Inc.
733 Third Avenue,
New York, NY 10017

© 1984 David Bell, Jeanne Bertrand,
Joy Hull, Oded Manor,
Denise Mumford, Bridget Walker

Printed and bound in Great Britain by
Robert Hartnoll Ltd. Bodmin, Cornwall

*British Library Cataloguing in
Publication Data*

Family work in action.—(Social
science paperbacks; no. 264)
1. Family social work
2. Family psychotherapy
I. Manor, Oded   II. Series
362.8'286   HV697
ISBN 0–422–78750–7
ISBN 0–422–78760–4   Pbk

*Library of Congress Cataloging in
Publication Data*

Main entry under title:

Family work in action.
   (Social science paperbacks; 264)
   Includes bibliographical references
   and indexes.
   1. Family social work—Great
   Britain—Case studies.
I. Manor, Oded.   II. Series.
HV700.G7F37 1984   362.8'253   84–533
ISBN 0–422–78750–7
ISBN 0–422–78760–4 (pbk.)

CONTENTS

PREFACE:
HOW THIS HANDBOOK
HAS COME ABOUT

Family work seemed to have taken root in the fieldwork section of Wandsworth social services by 1981. However, this was also a time of considerable upheaval and stress due to the reductions of staff and resources. Some of us, who had been involved in practice and training social workers for several years, recognized our own need to clear our heads and think about work. Sometime in the spring of that year discomfort led to action. Six of us began to meet once a month in the evenings in order to forward our own understanding of system theory. These reading seminars, over a glass of wine, gradually led to the formation of the present working group.

Someone asked 'where do we go from here?' and someone else calmly said 'I think we have enough material for a book'. We let this remain 'an idea' for quite a while. Yet it seemed to have stuck. As trainers we were acutely aware of the lack of a simple practice-oriented text that we could offer our training groups. We had all had to rely on a variety of material which, although relevant at some point, needed to be modified from the original clinical setting of family therapy to that of a social services department in a local authority office in Britain, where the term 'family work' is more appropriate. We felt that our work as trainers and supervisors could be made much simpler if there was such a text, and, as one of us put it, 'if nobody else is going to we'll have to do it ourselves'.

As we began to work on the layout of this book it appeared to be a good idea to weave our comments around one story. The Open University (1980) had already published a relevant case study with a family contributed by Oded Manor. The story of the Bailey family was a case study in focused family work which could easily be extended to demonstrate a variety of approaches. We selected the practice aspects we wanted to highlight and began to divide the sections among ourselves. A period of homework and group discussion followed. We have had to learn to accept criticism in the form of specific requests for alterations as well as praise from each other. We argued, laughed, survived heated discussions, but kept at it. The end product is the result of individual members taking responsibility for sections while incorporating many suggestions from the rest of the group (see Appendix II). We hope that our individuality has not been lost, but rather enriched by the fact that we have been working together in the same department, participating in many joint projects, and sharing our thoughts and feelings quite closely during the period of writing this handbook.

'. . . enough material for a book'

For convenience we have adopted the convention of referring to the family worker as 'she' and the client as 'he' throughout this book, except where specific cases are cited.

We would like to convey our warm thanks to all those who have supported and helped us: to our colleagues at the social services department of the London Borough of Wandsworth – fieldworkers, managers, and the training section, who are too numerous to be individually mentioned – we hope that their work is reflected honestly in the text; to Caroline Okell-Jones for her editorial assistance in presenting the original case study, in which Sue De Serville was student co-worker with Oded Manor; to Gwen Rosen who had the determination to go through this handbook as a whole and make suggestions about its literary shape; and to Tony Benjamin who offered his visual commentary in the cartoons. The editor would also like to thank Margaret Yelloly and Frank Ainsworth for expressing their confidence in the project and guiding it through to publication. The Open University was generous in allowing us to reproduce the transcript of the interviews with the Bailey family (Open University 1980). The School of Social Work at Middlesex Polytechnic offered crucial secretarial resources in the early stages.

David Bell, BA, Dip.Admin., Dip.App.Soc. Studies
Senior Social Worker, London Borough of Wandsworth

Jeanne Bertrand, BA, MS (Simmons USA)
Senior Social Worker, London Borough of Wandsworth

Joy Hull, Dip.Soc.Studies, AIMSW
Assistant Area Officer, London Borough of Wandsworth

Oded Manor, BA, PhD, Dip.App.Soc. Studies, Dip.Counselling
Senior Lecturer in Social Work, Middlesex Polytechnic (formerly
Senior Practitioner for Group Work, London Borough of Wandsworth)

Denise Mumford, BA, AIMSW
Training Officer, London Borough of Wandsworth

Bridget Walker, SRN, CQSW
Senior Social Worker, London Borough of Wandsworth

PART I
INTRODUCTION

Part I of this handbook sets out for the reader the preparatory work necessary before family work begins. This is done in three chapters: first, a brief 'Guide' is offered to later chapters; Chapter 2 takes an overview of system theory, the conceptual framework that underlies our thinking; Chapter 3 is more practical, aiming to help the reader make the transition into systemic thinking, and to prepare for later work with families.

1 / A GUIDE TO THIS HANDBOOK

It may help to read this guide before you approach the rest of the handbook. You will then know better what to expect and how the different chapters are organized.

This book is practice oriented: references are made to theory, but the emphasis is placed on the practical issues which arise when social workers apply family therapy skills to their work in a social services local authority office. This is not a recipe book: no 'pure' style is advocated. We have tried to explore a range of possibilities which are open to social workers when they work with families. You will meet a variety of styles; their choice was guided by two considerations: first, that they could be incorporated into a system theory approach and second, that they could be used by social workers in a local authority setting. Because of this combined approach we have preferred the term 'family work' rather than 'family therapy' in describing what we do. In this handbook you will find:

- one case of family work described in detail through all its phases
- descriptions of how family therapy techniques have been tailored to fit the particular requirements of a local authority setting – including its statutory duties
- a range of alternative interventions applied to the same family situation
- details of resources needed by workers including training, management support, and how to organize for them
- exercises to help you develop your own practice
- examples of how system theory can be applied in working with families in a local authority office
- suggestions for further reading about both practice and theory.

HOW THIS BOOK IS ORGANIZED

The book is divided into three parts:

Part I (Chapters 1–3) is introductory. Following this guide, Chapter 2 is a brief introduction to system theory as applied to the family. Chapter 3 deals in some detail with the preparatory work required of an individual or a group wanting to work systemically with families.

Part II (Chapters 4–11) describes in detail the work with one family, the Baileys (a synopsis is provided at the start to help you grasp the whole plot more easily). The phases of working with the Baileys are presented first (Chapter 4) and then the full story is related as it emerged interview by interview (Chapters 5–10). The phases and the interventions are part of a framework we call 'focused family work'. At appropriate points we interrupt the story to comment on practice issues which tend to arise at that stage of the work. These comments are made from a variety of angles, some rather different from that of the main story. They are given under the same heading:

(a) A summary of what the workers did in the interview;
(b) Suggestions as to how else that situation could have been handled;
(c) Discussion of a relevant practice issue;
(d) A different case example related to the practice issue (c);
(e) Activities for further learning.

Part III (Chapters 12–14) starts with an exploration of our failures (Chapter 12). Many of the earlier examples are of cases that went well, and we thought it important to share our thoughts about some of the difficulties we have encountered. Chapter 13 is dedicated to discussing training and supervision in terms of content and process as well as the organization needed to provide them in a local authority office. The final chapter (Chapter 14) reaches outside work with families to other situations in which social workers are involved and to which systemic concepts are relevant, for example adoption and fostering.

This book is designed to help you improve your practice. In addition to reading it privately and reflecting on the material, you may find it helpful to share it, section by section, with a colleague or a supervision group. However you use it, we hope you enjoy the material and particularly the exercises. After all learning seems most likely to occur when you also have a good time.

2 / THEORY BEFORE PRACTICE

There is considerable interest in family work among social workers today but few social work courses include more than one or two lectures on the subject, and many social workers were trained in a different method and find the transition to systemic thinking difficult.

We hope that readers who follow the main guidelines in this book will be helped to make the transition from working with individuals (perhaps in a family context) to working with the family as a system, which in our view is often a more effective approach to family problems. In this introductory chapter we start by defining family therapy, and then set out a short statement of its theory to explain the theoretical base from which we work.

WHAT IS FAMILY THERAPY?

Family therapy is an intervention for change in a natural system, the family. The definition of Beels (1969) in his helpful overview of schools of family therapy, is worth consideration. He first sets out the key elements of individual psychotherapy:

'(a) There are two people in confidential interaction.
(b) The mode of interaction is usually verbal.
(c) The interaction is relatively prolonged; and
(d) The relationship has for a definite and agreed-upon purpose changes in the behaviour in one of the participants.'

He then applies these considerations to family therapy:

'(a) There are more than two people, and the communication between them is open.

(b) Non-verbal interaction assumes a primary importance along with the verbal.
(c) It is often shorter than individual therapy, but this is enormously variable.
(d) The relationship has for its definite and agreed upon purpose *changes in the family system* of interaction, not changes in the behaviour of individuals. Individual change occurs as a by-product of system change.'

(Beels 1969: 283)

Point (d) is underlined because of its key importance.

HISTORICAL DEVELOPMENT

In the field of psychiatry, the first four decades of the century were taken up mainly with the development of individual therapy. During the 1940s there was a rapid development of interest in the dynamics of small and large groups. Between 1950 and 1960 the early work in family therapy of the Palo Alto Group, all of whom worked with adults suffering from schizophrenia, was taking place in the USA. The movement towards working with family groups in this country was slower to develop. The lead

Social workers were working with families long before family group work became common in psychiatric circles.

was taken by Dr Robin Skynner at Woodbury Down Clinic during the 1960s. His articles printed in *Social Work Today* in 1971 were very influential in social work circles, and his pioneer work at the Institute of Group Analysis in the provision of an introductory course in family therapy (later organized by the Institute of Family Therapy) has provided basic training in family therapy for many social workers during the last decade. The contributors to this book have been much influenced by the work in family therapy at the Tavistock Clinic and at the Family Institute, Cardiff, and also by such great international therapists as Satir, Minuchin, and the Milan group (Hoffman 1981).

Social workers were working with families long before family group work became common in psychiatric circles. Even in 1903 (see Smith 1965) the training of social workers in the Charity Organization Society included lectures on the family as a unit of social life. In family agencies, such as the Family Welfare Association and Family Service Units, social workers saw family groups together as a matter of course and were aware at a practical level of the ways in which the family system works. They lacked a coherent theory, and were somewhat distracted by the introduction of psycho-analytically-oriented casework in the 1960s which, while providing many insights into the understanding of individual problems, shifted attention from the family group for a time. However, from the mid 1970s systemic ideas were available to all and family casework changed into family therapy.

THE FAMILY AS A SYSTEM

Families have been studied from many directions but for the purposes of this book we choose to discuss the systemic approach only. The brief statement of theory below is intended to provide readers with some knowledge of the theoretical base accepted by all contributors to this manual. As it is a practice manual, we have cut the theoretical content to a minimum. The next few pages are not adequate to teach the basic tenets of system theory; we make recommendations for further reading in Appendix I.

A primary function of a family is to support the development of its members

It does this by carrying out:

   (i) Basic tasks – the provision of food, shelter, etc.
  (ii) Development tasks – enhancing individual development and transition through the life stages.
 (iii) Hazardous tasks – dealing with loss of income, sudden death, etc.

The boundaries of the family system

   (i) The family is a system which has a sense of its own identity.
  (ii) Family members are aware of the family boundary, that is who is inside the family, and who is not. The boundary can change to include new members (e.g.

step-parents) or exclude others (e.g. the black sheep) but only with considerable stress.

(iii) The system contains sub-systems such as the marital pair and sibling group.

(iv) The family acts as a sub-system of other systems (e.g. the extended family, or neighbourhood).

(v) Families vary in the degree to which they operate as 'closed' or 'open' systems. In other words, some families are much more involved with the community, friends, and neighbours, than others. No living systems are entirely closed.

(vi) Families also vary in the pace at which they are able to absorb change (Olson, Sprenkle, and Russel 1979).

The concept of 'fit' in relation to family behaviour

(i) The behaviour of all family members is related to and dependent upon other family members. Actions of individuals in the family are constantly reinforced when they fit with those of others in that particular family; behaviours which do not fit receive no reinforcement and therefore tend not to recur. Over time regular patterns of behaviour emerge.

(ii) The behaviour of different individuals within the system fits together in a meaningful whole. A simple example of this is the 'nag – withdraw – nag' cycle; he withdraws because she nags; she nags because he withdraws. Neither of these behaviours causes the other; they are part of a circular pattern. The concept of 'fit' better describes behaviour within the system model than the concept of 'cause and effect'. Andolfi argues that 'the formulation of problems in terms of cause and effect is the result of an arbitrary punctuation of a circular situation, which isolates an event from the sequence of events which precede and follow it' (Andolfi 1979: 1). The idea of fit is central to the family system model.

The family system is more than the sum of its components

(i) 'Beyond the parts, there appears a new entity; an organism, multi-bodied and purposeful, whose parts are regulated by the rules of the whole' (Minuchin and Fishman 1981: 193). In order to understand this idea it is necessary to take an overall view of a family from different angles, like seeing both sides of the coin and the surface between. It is impossible to do this from within the system itself. Individuals within the family are bound to see things from their own points of view, although they are aware of the larger whole and the power of its influence.

(ii) The total family system consists of its *components* (family members), their *attributes* (personal characteristics), and the *interaction* between them. We may begin with the example of information exchange: in a chain passing information from A to D, each link is modified and changed by its interaction. This modification occurs in a circular process known as a 'feedback loop' – ultimately the last point on the chain is fed-back to the first point: a–b; b1–c;

c1−d; d1−a; a1−, etc. As cross-communication occurs (e.g. from b to d, etc.) more complex spirals of exchange are created. These are well illustrated in some of the poems of R. D. Laing (1970). The information changes the people and the people change the information, while performing different functions that sustain the system as a whole (Kantor and Lehr 1975).

Change in the family system

(i) Inputs into the family system (by family members or from the environment) are modified by the system. 'A stimulus does not cause a process to occur in an otherwise inert system. It merely modifies processes already existing in an autonomously active system' (Bertalanffy 1968).

(ii) The family is a relatively stable system which adapts through feedback to meet the changing developmental needs of its members, as well as adjusting to environmental changes. It maintains itself in a condition of 'dynamic equilibrium between two seemingly contradictory functions: a tendency towards homeostasis (a steady state) and a capacity for transformation' (Andolfi 1979: 7).

(iii) The interaction processes which tend to *restore* existing patterns of behaviour that have been disturbed are called *'negative feedback' mechanisms*. All families which stay together are characterized by some degree of stability (homeostasis or steady state) in their patterns of behaviour. However, some families have rather rigid patterns of communication and tend to move too readily towards a steady state so that they cannot adapt to change.

(iv) Interaction processes which lead to *change* and to the development of individuals within the system are called *'positive feedback' mechanisms*.

(v) Dell (1982: 32) suggests that 'the system cannot behave without altering itself'. Every interaction within a family system leaves some mark on the family. However, for long periods of time the family changes only within a limited range. It could be said to stay in the same gear. The minor changes within a family such as a child learning to dress herself or a parent to drive a car affect all members to some degree but disrupt family life relatively little. They are marked by a sense of achievement and members experience no substantial alteration in identity. These piecemeal changes within the system are sometimes called 'first order changes' (Watzlawick, Weakland, and Fisch 1974).

(vi) More significant changes happen infrequently. 'At the level of first order phenomena the family is constantly evolving, while at the level of second order phenomena it is episodically reformed' (Terkelsen 1980: 40). The events listed below usually require substantial adjustment within the family system:

(a) major changes outside the nuclear family, e.g. war or recession
(b) changes in family of origin, e.g. death of a grandparent
(c) a member enters or leaves the nuclear family, e.g. divorce of parents
(d) biological changes, e.g. adolescence
(e) major social changes initiated by the family, e.g. family moves abroad.

The adjustment to these changes may require a re-assignment of roles within the family and changes in the meaning of relationships. To meet the new needs 'very basic attributes of the family unit must change. Ultimately the family's prior system of meaning gives way under the advance of a new shared reality' (Terkelsen 1980). This kind of second order change requires a leap to a new integration of the system, like a shift to a higher gear, or a change in the rules of a game. When behaviours are charged with new meaning, *'meta feedback' mechanisms* operate in the family.

DIFFICULTIES, SYMPTOMS, AND DYSFUNCTIONAL BEHAVIOUR

(i) In traditional individual psychotherapy, symptoms and problematic behaviour are seen as an expression of conflicts *within* the individual: a patient might talk about 'my depression', seeing it as an expression of his/her inner world. In contrast, family therapists try to understand symptomatic behaviour within the context of the family system. (In an interview with a young couple – seen on one of his videotapes – Minuchin asks the wife who is complaining of depression, *'Who* is depressing you?' Instead of dwelling on her feelings, he is leading her towards an interactional view of her behaviour with her husband.)

(ii) Difficulties are tackled by families every day with varying degrees of success. Family therapists think that difficulties only turn into problems or symptoms when the solution sought by the family is too rigid (that is used repeatedly regardless of its effect) or extreme. Problems are likely to become severe when the family fails to accommodate to second order changes. These are concerned with the developmental needs of individuals and the progress of the family through its life stages and other significant periods of transition. Frustration of these developments is likely to lead to worse symptoms than frustration of first order changes; parents may disapprove of *one* of their daughter's boyfriends; the resulting family conflict is likely to be less severe than if they tried to prevent their daughter having *any* relationships with the opposite sex.

(iii) It is helpful to question the function of the symptom within the family system. It is often possible to understand how a symptom which brings great distress to one individual may be saving others in the family from facing severe anxieties. The 'good daughter' who remains at home as mother's companion may be keeping her parents at a safe distance from each other. Her phobia about leaving the house may be a lesser evil to the family than the fear of conflict or divorce between the parents which could be the fantasized alternatives if they are left alone together. We can ask the question in a different way, 'What might happen within the family if they did not have this symptom?' If we understand the positive value which a symptom holds within a family system, we can help the family to let go of the symptom and find a more constructive way of meeting their need.

THE PURPOSE OF FAMILY THERAPY

Family therapy is about helping distressed individuals who are showing symptoms or self-defeating behaviours within the context of the family. The means of doing this is by helping the family as a system to deal with whatever change of family relationships is required to promote a more satisfactory fit, thus affording the chance of development for its individual members. The remainder of this book deals with the practical issues involved in helping families to achieve this kind of change.

3 / A PERIOD OF PREPARATION

In this chapter we suggest ways for the reader to prepare for doing systems work with families. Most people find the incentive to read about family therapy, discuss the ideas, and learn about techniques, from their work with real families whom they want to help. However, during the early stages of learning a new theory, most of us become muddled and tend to be more uncertain in our work for a while. For this reason, we believe that a planned period of preparation is helpful, in order to assimilate the theory as thoroughly as possible before attempting to put it into practice with families in need. This period of preparation could take anything between two to six months and should not be hurried. The outline below can easily be developed into an introductory course.

We see the period of preparation as having four phases:

phase A – Starting a group
phase B – Sharing the theory
phase C – Integrating the theory
phase D – Preparing the group for family work.

PHASE A – STARTING A GROUP

We do not believe it is realistic to try to begin family work alone. The stimulus, the support, and the opportunity for feedback which another person or a group can provide are necessary. The first requirement is to set up a small group of like-minded colleagues. A group of four or six people is ideal as a starting point although if there is only one other person in your area who is interested in family work, it is viable to practise as a pair.

You may have worked with members of your group already, or you may be relative strangers to each other. Even if you think you know each other well, it is worthwhile trying to spend some time together in an informal atmosphere – go out for a drink, or have lunch together. Discuss common interests at work and also share something about your life at home.

TASK: the exercises below are designed to help the members of the group to work together better:

First choose a partner, then

(a) Write down three things which you want your partner to know about you and share these together. Be positive about yourself. Then change over and let your partner have a turn.

Write down three things which you fear your partner will find out about you. Tell your partner what reactions you fear most when this happens, then change over. Discuss between you what support you need and how to ensure it is there.

(b) Write down what you personally wish to achieve from working in the group. Share your objectives with the others, and attempt to set group objectives. Keep your list and check it at regular intervals to see whether you are achieving what you set out to do. Alter your objectives if necessary at a later date.

(c) Provide yourselves with large sheets of paper, felt pens, toys (play people, farm animals, etc). Take some paper and draw the route which has led to your present membership of the group. Be imaginative in the way you express this. Indicate by drawings/words/symbols why you have moved towards a special interest in work with families. Share your 'maps' with each other.

Going back to your own family

Some groups have found it useful to talk with each other about their families of origin, although at present this is not a standard part of family therapy training. There are those who feel that it should be (Lieberman 1982) and there is a very strong case for social workers to have the opportunity to deal with some of the unfinished business from their families of origin *before* starting to help with the problems of other families. Good experiences in the group working with members' families can greatly strengthen trust and cohesiveness and are a good preliminary to co-working partnerships.

However, this sort of work should only be undertaken if there is a clear commitment in the group; no one should feel obliged to participate. It can be helpful to have an outside consultant to lead the group during these sessions.

Geneograms. One way of exploring the family of origin is by preparing a family tree. Some people are already guardians of their family history and know an enormous amount about their families and about earlier generations. Others may know little, and have to turn to relatives to fill in the gaps. This is not always an easy process; some families are very scattered, or key relatives are already dead. Sometimes close relatives may be surprisingly cagey in talking about the family. (For example, a colleague found that his mother refused to talk about her parents, and he had to find out about them from another source – a distant cousin.) Many families have reasons for keeping things secret or having a 'cover story' for painful episodes, but uncovering the past can bring great relief to us, and explain half understood prohibitions or requirements handed down through the family.

Understanding the themes and myths from our families of origin is fascinating but it stirs up emotions and is sometimes painful; considerable support should be offered by the group to each individual who talks about his/her family, and plenty of time set aside for the discussion. Members of the group may be able to point out issues which would escape the individual; for example, when a colleague first did a geneogram, it was noticed that she had left out her father's surname, while naming everyone in her mother's family. This led her to think about her relationship with her father, who had died when she was an infant. Over the next two years she started to search out information and explore her fantasies about him. In the context of this book, what is of prime importance is the way that our relations with our families of origin affect our work; through her geneogram this colleague learned to give better balance to the contribution of the father in the household.

Doing a geneogram also helps us to recognize how blocks in our work with families can relate to issues in our families of origin. We may need to go back to relatives and talk with them in a new way (adult to adult) before we can sort out these difficulties.

Work on a geneogram can be started in the group, and carried out by the individual over a period of time, with report back sessions at intervals. For further ideas about the use of geneograms, read Lieberman (1982).

Family sculpture. Another way of working with your family of origin is through family sculpting. You can choose a scene from the past which is either typical of your family, or may be puzzling in some way, and portray the family relationships through a tableau vivant. You need, 'the sculptor, who risks to reveal his private view; *the monitor* who guides the sculptor towards clarity and definition; and the *actors* who lead themselves to portray members of the sculptor's system only as the sculptor sees them' (Duhl, Kantor, and Duhl 1973: 53). You can also use observers of the whole process. There is emphasis on space – distance and closeness between family members; posture and movements – the way an individual typically expresses him/herself non-verbally; and expression – typical affect. The sculpture can be mobile or static. After experiencing the tableau for a few moments, the sculptor may reach some new insight about his/her family; or more typically this will come later as the actors feed back their reactions to the roles they have played. The monitor may need to provide space for the sculptor to explore his/her own memories or may gently give a lead towards a different view of the family. For learning more about sculpting read Papp, Silverstein, and Carter (1973).

PHASE B – SHARING THE THEORY

After the support group has been set up, and some work has been done on the members' families of origin, the next step is to learn about system theory. The group can be used for a period as a reading seminar. Some suggestions for preliminary reading are included in Appendix I. A way of starting is suggested below:

TASK: each member of the group prepares notes on ONE chapter from the following list or equivalent texts (including preparation of visual aids):

(a) Chapter 2: 'Theoretical frameworks', in S. Walrond-Skinner (1976) *Family Therapy*.
(b) Introduction: 'The family, as an interactional system', in M. Andolfi (1979) *Family Therapy: An Interactional Approach*.
(c) Chapter 1: 'Systems, order, hierarchy', in A. C. R. Skynner (1976) *One Flesh, Separate Persons*.

Then in groups of about three, each person discusses the basic points of his/her chapter with the other two, taking a maximum of thirty minutes to do so. This is followed by half an hour of general discussion.

It is helpful to try to translate the jargon into your own words and to use analogies and illustrations to make the complex ideas as interesting and straightforward as possible.

Example 1. Give the following quotations to the group and ask them to explain how they illustrate systems ideas.

— 'All parts of an organism form a circle. Therefore, every part is both beginning and end.' (Hippocrates)
— Judge to Whore: 'You have to be a delinquent. If you are not a delinquent, I cannot be a judge.' (Jean Genet, *The Balcony*)
— 'No man is an island entire of itself: everyman is a piece of the Continent, a part of the Maine.' (John Donne, *Devotions*)

Example 2. Consider the following chess problem:

(a) Define the 'individual' powers of the Black Queen, the most versatile piece on the chess board (*Figure 1(a)*).
(b) Now consider the position of the Black Queen in the chess board system (*Figure 1(b)*).

Figure 1 The powers of the Black Queen

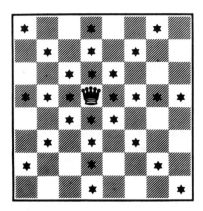

(a)

(b)

In one move the Queen may go to any square marked: ·

The Queen is pinned and helpless, for to move it from the diagonal would expose the King to check.

This task could be extended by comparing the chess example with a real family. For example, the King might be compared with a father who is protected by all other family members because of his heart condition. Systemic ideas may be hard to follow at first, but they do not have to be boring.

At the end of this task group members should be able to define or describe the following:

(a) the system is more than its parts
(b) homeostatis
(c) positive feedback
(d) a permeable boundary.

It is worth getting help from an experienced colleague to plan a series of reading seminars over a period of months. Below is a suggested outline which we have used ourselves:

1 System theory
2 The family life cycle
3 Theories of change
4 Different schools of family therapy (e.g. communication, structural, strategic, etc.)

5 Techniques of family therapy
6 Practical issues:
   – preparing the referral network
   – the first session
   – dealing with resistance
   – working with young children in the family group
   – maintaining the process of change
7 Co-therapy
8 Supervision and training.

The recommended books in Appendix I cover most of the issues above, at least in a preliminary way.

PHASE C – INTEGRATING THE THEORY

After gaining an intellectual grasp of the theory, it needs to be integrated in practice. The social worker who is a systemic thinker has a very different framework for making sense of families from someone who is primarily concerned with the individual. Acquiring a different framework is hard work and cannot be done quickly; it may take about two years.

In this section we are concerned to help the reader faced with a family group to begin to observe individuals within the *context* of their environment. The importance of context is illustrated by the following example.

Watzlawick *et al.* quote Konrad Lorenz who was seen by some tourists dragging himself, crouching, round a meadow in figures of eight, quacking like a duck. The tourists appeared horrified and must have thought Lorenz had taken leave of his senses. They could not see the ducklings following him in the long grass – he was doing an imprinting experiment with himself as mother substitute. The authors comment that 'Failure to realize the intricacies of the relationship between an event and the matrix in which it takes place, between an organism and its environment, either confronts the observer with something "mysterious" or induces him to attribute to his object of study certain properties the object may not possess' (Watzlawick, Beavin, and Jackson 1967: 21). In order to understand individuals in difficulties, therefore, we need to observe them in their environment: the family, the peer group, the work setting, etc, depending on the nature of their problem. In this book we concentrate on the family context, although the influence of other social groups can be equally important.

For a beginner, working with a family often creates a sense of buzzing confusion. It is important, therefore, to build up a systemic framework which provides some guidelines for what to observe, and what to make of these observations.

Your aims should be:

(i) to improve your skill in observing *non-verbal* communication;
(ii) to observe patterns of communication *between* people and *sequences* of behaviour;

(iii) to attempt to identify the *positive value* that distressing behaviours have for a family group.

Learning to observe non-verbal communication

Communications are made at two different levels. When trying to understand family behaviour we should not only *listen* to what is said, but also *watch* for the movements and expression which accompany the message. What is said is described as the *content* or *report* aspect of the communication; the *command* aspect refers to how the communication is to be taken, and indicates something about the relationship involved. This is indicated in the following:

FRIEND: 'Get to the pub this minute and fetch some beer': the report message is a verbal account, and is also a command message of an order to do it. If it is accompanied by a smile, the report message would be the same but the command message would be:
'I'm only joking'.

or

PARENT: 'Would you have the time to go to the corner shop for me?': the report message is a simple question. If it is accompanied by a frown, the command message would be an order to do it.

The variations are endless.

Many of the families with whom we are involved are characterized by a constant struggle about the nature of their relationships, and the command aspect of their communications swamps that of the report. Often the report and command aspects are not congruent. An ability to notice *both* levels of communication, however subtly the command element is expressed, is an essential in family work.

An observer can only pay attention to a limited amount of data at one time. He/she will be more likely to notice sudden or dramatic changes of behaviour, for example, someone bursting into tears or shouting. It is important, however, to improve the capacity for noticing detail: a slight shift in body posture or the movement of the head. Noticing the details is the first stage. A family worker also needs confidence in drawing attention to non-verbal behaviour, of which members of a group may be unaware. The significance of a sequence of behaviour is not always apparent straight away, but the therapist may sense that it is somehow important. For example, in a family whose elder son was about to have an operation for the removal of a lump from his thigh, the mother was telling the worker that her son was not anxious about going into hospital. The worker noticed that the two boys were biting a long piece of Plasticine. This game was accompanied by excited laughter, which helped to draw the worker's attention to it. They talked about the game, and the mother mentioned proudly that the boy had been drawing a picture of a crocodile, with beautifully modelled teeth 'like knives'. This enabled the boy to talk about his fear of the surgeon's knife.

TASK: try this task in your group to help you improve your capacity to notice non-verbal communication:

Show a short film, preferably one involving children. (For example, *John*, by the Robertsons, produced by the Tavistock Institute of Human Relations.) It is better to choose a film that members of the group have seen before, so that they are not too curious about the content. Play it without sound and watch very carefully. This can be organized in different ways: (a) each person observes for one minute then spends three minutes noting down what he/she has seen; then watches again for a minute. Afterwards group members compare notes and discuss similarities and differences in what they have noticed; (b) alternatively, it may be helpful for each group member to identify with an individual on the screen, watch his/her behaviour closely, and then compare notes with the others who have observed different characters.

Observing patterns of behaviour between people

'A family is a system which operates through transactional patterns. Repeated transactions establish patterns of how, when and to whom to relate and these patterns underpin the system. When a mother tells her child to drink his juice and he obeys, this transaction defines who he is in relation to her, in that context and at that time. Repeated operations in these terms constitute a transactional pattern.'

(Minuchin 1974: 52)

When we watch a family (unlike a stranger group) we have to remember that these intricate patterns have been established for years. Their origin 'is buried in years of explicit and implicit negotiations among family members, often around small daily events' (Minuchin 1974). The observer of a family needs to identify these repetitive patterns in order to understand the relationships in the family.

Noticing a sequence of behaviour on one occasion does not mean that the behaviour is typical of the family group. It is always necessary to check out with the family whether this behaviour occurs regularly or to notice yourself whether it is repeated. For example, on one occasion a worker became aware that a mother was talking a great deal to her daughter (3) and less to the toddler (1½). To test her original observation she made a note of the number of times the mother communicated with each child: in fact she communicated with the elder more than double the number of times that she communicated with the younger. Here is a typical description:

Enid (1½) was eating a banana. It was sticking straight out of her mouth and she played her fingers up and down as though it was a wind instrument. She was sucking on the banana, very concentrated and self-contained. Mother was leaning with both elbows on the table, chin in her hands looking at Patsy (3). She said 'You can drink it now'. Patsy looked at her mother, picked up her cup and took a drink of soup. She smiled. Mother asked 'Was that nice?'

The behaviour of this triad was a transactional pattern and reflected their normal relationships with each other. (In fact, Enid had an exceptionally close relationship with her father, who had taken on many of the nurturing tasks with her.)

Inexperienced observers will inevitably notice those elements of behaviour which relate to their understanding of family life, based primarily on their own experience in their family of origin. In order to correct this sort of bias, it is helpful to use a set framework for a period. A number of researchers have developed scales for the appraisal of the functioning of family groups, such as Walsh (1982) and a good but very detailed scale was developed by Behrens et al. (1969). Below is a simple format under three headings which you might use when observing a family group:

Communication
Atmosphere
Boundaries

Communication
Notice pathways of communication
  – eye contact between family members;
  – the direction of gestures;
  – the movement of people in the group;
  – who talks *to* whom?
  – who talks *for* whom?
Notice the clarity of communications.
Notice the congruence between verbal and non-verbal messages.
What is the frequency and type of control messages – questions, orders, etc?
How does the family deal with conflicts, expressions of feeling, etc?
Who initiates the discussion of what topic? Who responds, who is left out, who distracts attention from the topic?

Atmosphere
Notice mood of family when together.
Notice mood of individual members
  – how well are the differences between individuals recognized?
What is the tone of communications?
  – does family show affection and appreciation?
  – is behaviour largely attacking or argumentative?
  – what is the range of feelings expressed?
Is humour part of the family experience?
What sort of laughter is heard?

Boundaries
How clear are the roles in the family?

– parent/child
– husband/wife
– grandparent/parent

How appropriate are the roles for this family's life stage?

What is the degree of differentiation between individuals, sexes, and generations?

Consider the level of intrusion, interference, exclusion, or disconnectedness in relation to different family members.

What are the coalitions in the family?

TASK

(a) If you have access to video equipment make a short videotape of a family involved in an activity together. You can use a client family, or that of a friend or acquaintance unknown to your group who may agree to help with this. Choose a family with at least two children, preferably aged 3–10. Shuffle a pack of cards and ask the family to set the cards out on a table in order of numbers and suits. The only other instruction is that all members of the family must join in the task. The family is given five minutes to complete this exercise.

(b) Show the videotape to your group. After watching the tape each group member makes notes on what he/she has seen, using the outline above. Discuss your findings together. Show the tape again and check your evidence.

If your department does not own video equipment it is worth exploring other local resources (such as the education department).

When you start working with families it is helpful to use regularly an observation format, on which the group have agreed, to help develop a sound internal framework (that is, a capacity for knowing spontaneously what to look for) for the assessment of family behaviour.

Mutuality

It is essential to notice another aspect of transactional patterns: their mutuality. The 'nag – withdraw – nag' cycle can just as properly be expressed 'withdraw – nag – withdraw'. The typical exchange is reinforced on all sides – if someone alters the pattern, another person will pull it back into shape. Here is an example from the family mentioned earlier, in which the older child has a closer relationship with the mother than the younger one.

Patsy (3) was roaming around the room, refusing to settle down and eat her meal. Enid (1½) had already finished and was playing with a glove puppet. Mother picked up Enid and offered her a bite of toast. Immediately Patsy came and sat up at the table. She took the glove puppet from Enid. Enid yelled out and mother became preoccupied with getting Patsy to hand over the puppet. Enid got down from the table and wandered off into the other room. As soon as mother's eyes were on Enid, Patsy came back and claimed her attention and mother equally quickly responded. Enid accepted the situation and withdrew.

Although it is tempting to see one person (usually an adult) as the initiator in a sequence of behaviour, it is not helpful to think in terms of cause and effect once a transactional pattern is established. A habitual way of behaving, even when apparently painful for one of the participants, has a strong hold on the whole group.

TASK

In pairs one person act the 'nagging wife' and another the 'withdrawn husband'. Do this first in dumb show — both should indicate by gesture what they want for themselves from the other. After five minutes, introduce words and continue acting these two parts for another five minutes. Move into the group and feedback how one person's behaviour affected the other, and vice versa. De-role carefully after this exercise. You can try this with different 'pairs' (for example, anxious mother and delinquent son); or you can introduce a third person into the pair and observe the difference in behaviour. (In all sculpting or role-play exercises, try not to 'act'. Throw yourself into the part using any experience you have had or know about. Try to describe your own feelings after the exercise, rather than saying 'I think this person may have felt . . .'.)

The positive value of distressing behaviour within the system

It is hard to understand the persistence of some behaviours within the family which seem on the face of it to be causing distress, pain, anger, and other uncomfortable emotions, but to which family members cling with tenacity. Instead of seeing such behaviour as merely problematic, it seems helpful to hypothesize about what positive value the behaviour might have within the system. This involves 'the gentle art of reframing': 'To reframe means to change the conceptual and/or emotional setting or viewpoint in relation to which a situation is experienced and to place it in another frame which fits the "facts" of the same concrete situation equally well or even better, and thereby changes its whole meaning' (Watzlawick, Weakland, and Fisch 1974: 92–109).

QUESTION: What is the difference between an optimist and a pessimist?

ANSWER: The optimist says of a glass that is half full: the pessimist says of the same glass that is half empty.

If we act as optimists at times in our view of human behaviour, it enormously extends our understanding. In terms of individual behaviour let us take the example provided by Susie Orbach (1978) who asks fat women to consider the *positive* value of their fat; 'Getting fat is a very definite and purposeful act connected to women's social position.' These are some of the good things that women said about their fat:

fat represented concrete strength;

- acted as a protection;
- made the person feel big and warm.

Harriet (35) is quoted, 'I had the feeling that my fat gives me substance and physical presence in the world. It allows me to do all the things I have to do. In the fantasy I saw myself in my office sitting at my desk and taking up an enormous amount of space. I felt the capacity to do what I needed to do – challenge my boss and fight more effectively for the community group that I'm here to serve. I felt my strength in this exaggeration of my size' (Orbach 1978: 44).

Let us examine a simple family example: John (7) has stopped attending school. He is referred to social services because of his school problems. He is the elder of two boys. His younger brother is lively and cheerful and is managing in playgroup with no difficulty. Father has a regular job and takes the boys swimming at weekends. Mother devotes herself entirely to her home and family. Her father, who lived with the family, died a year ago. We might make the following hypothesis about the value of John's 'symptomatic' behaviour within his family group: John is a shy boy who is very attached to his mother and currently finds more satisfaction in the comfort of his home than he does at school; his brother has the satisfaction of developing normally within his peer group, without pressure from his mother and with father's support and praise. The mother was very attached to her father and misses him. John's presence at home makes her life full and comfortable although at one level she is anxious that he is so 'shy'. Father felt pressure from his wife to give her more attention and emotional commitment after her father's death. Now through John's care for his mother, father is able to return to his previous comfortable distance in his relations to his wife. He still has the satisfaction of knowing that his youngest son is a 'real boy'.

There may be other reasons why this family has struck difficulties now. Perhaps mother never fully separated from her family of origin when she married. In her fantasy she still needs a father to care for her. Perhaps one or both parents have anxiety about 'becoming independent' because of some myth in their family of origin. This too might explain why they are having difficulty moving to the next life stage with children at school. Anyone intervening in this family must be aware of the resistance which is likely to arise when the family is asked to help John back into school. The resistance is tied up with the value of John's behaviour to the whole family. Who will attend to mother's grief if John goes back to school? How will the two boys manage their competition for father's approval? Although we are only making a hypothesis about an imaginary family, it is possible to go through a similar process with real families which are known to us. The validity of the hypothesis can then be checked out by questions and observation (Palazzoli *et al.* 1980).

TASK

Now is the time to start using your group for real case discussions. First read together and discuss Palazzoli *et al.* (1980), then take a family already known to you and ask the appropriate questions about the central problem. Try to hypothesize about what value this behaviour has to this family group.

Avoid all negative language. You may only hypothesize about the *positive* value of the symptomatic behaviour. List each family member and make a statement about the possible value of the behaviour to that person.

PHASE D – PREPARING TO USE THE GROUP AS A FAMILY WORKSHOP

In your group so far you have been through three stages:

(a) defining the objectives of the group and learning to work together;
(b) reading some basic texts about family therapy and sharing them with each other;
(c) building a new internal framework (based on family systems theory) for assessment of families.

We suggest a further stage of preparation before you start family work yourself. At this point you should view as many videotapes as possible of families in therapy. You should decide what supervision you will need and make plans for this. Finally, you should decide whether you wish to do co-therapy and if so, do some preparatory work with a partner.

There are two main ways of seeing family work in action. The first is to watch videotapes of interviews. For example, it is possible to hire tapes from the Institute of Family Therapy, London. You may also find that colleagues in a nearby agency or hospital have been using video in their work with families and are willing to negotiate for you to view one or more of their tapes. It can be counter-productive to watch too many 'experts' at work; you may feel 'I can never do as well as that; I had better give up now'. However, to watch one or two sessions in which a family is helped by a good family worker is very inspiring. Conferences are occasionally held at which well-known practitioners present their work and these offer another opportunity to see family work in progress with the additional advantage of the worker explaining his/her approach in person.

Another way of watching process is to sit behind a one-way screen while a family is interviewed (Cornwell and Pearson 1981.) This may be more difficult to arrange than the hire of a video tape; but there are some centres where you can enrol as a student and attend throughout the work with one family, joining in discussions about the process of work.

Although it is preferable to *see* a family interview, there are a number of books which provide detailed transcripts of family interviews, with comments on the process (e.g. Haley and Hoffman 1967). By both seeing and reading about family work it is possible to get a first impression of what is good practice.

Supervision. Is essential if your work is to improve (see Chapter 13). At this stage you need to make plans for the regular supervision of your group. You may decide that you can offer each other adequate feedback and advice. The usual forum for group expression in social work agencies is the 'case discussion'. Since a good deal of your work with families will depend on understanding the family system, experiential exercises, such as family sculpting, may be useful (Walrond-Skinner 1976). It is better still to show videotapes of your family interviews to each other, having gained the family's permission to do so. You can then spend time carefully watching short extracts in order to make a hypothesis about the family, based on much more objective data than a social worker can give in a verbal report. You can offer better advice about the social worker's interventions because you have seen them with your own eyes. See if you can negotiate the regular use of video equipment for this purpose. Audio-tape is a good second best to video and most social workers own small cassette recorders. Few families object to their use in sessions.

If you feel that your group needs more expert supervision than the members are able to offer each other, you may be able to persuade your training department to finance some sessions with an outside consultant. Obviously you should first look for expert help from within your own agency. Ideally, family work is developed within teams or area groups (see Chapter 13) and you may have a team leader or colleague who is more experienced than yourselves and can be called upon as a group leader. If you need to look outside the agency for help, it is important to discuss this in detail with your team leader or section head. He/she is accountable to the agency for your casework and has a right to know what you are doing in your work with families. If there is trust between a worker and supervisor, based on the knowledge that they are both concerned for the good of the client and committed to the work of the agency, this is not an insuperable problem. In our experience team leaders are usually flexible about allowing social workers to develop aspects of their work with colleagues. It should be acceptable for you to consult with the Fostering and Adoption Unit about the placement of a child or to discuss with the Intermediate Treatment section (IT) ways of involving an adolescent with the peer group. There is nothing sinister about developing new skills, particularly when they prove to be effective. The main requirement is to share your plans with management from the start and where possible, to involve a member of the management team in your group.

Co-Working. In your early work with families you may find it a great support to have a co-worker. This is particularly true when the family is large or disruptive and while you are finding your way in the work. However, co-work can become an extra problem rather than a strength unless you have done a great deal of work on your relationship with your partner. If you have both been members of the group during the period of preparation, you will now know each other quite well but will still need time to make a partnership in your family work (Hannum 1980).

TASK

Talk together about your differences:
- **in professional experience;**
- **in working style;**
- **levels of seniority;**
- **age/sex/marital status;**
- **in families of origin.**

Perhaps the most important work of preparation is in building a relationship of trust and openness which will allow a dialogue about *differences of opinion* – in other words, how well do you disagree?

It may take your group several months of preparation to reach this point if you follow the suggestions noted above. That may seem a long time; but you have a greater chance of helping families if you are confident in the orientation to your work.

PART II
WORK WITH THE
BAILEY* FAMILY

The second part of this book (Chapters 4–11) is a session by session account of working with one family: the Baileys. At various points we interrupt the narrative to comment on practice issues which tend to arise at that phase of the work:

— *we summarize the workers' activities;*
— *examine alternatives;*
— *raise general issues related to this stage of the work;*
— *offer other case examples; and*
— *suggest activities for future learning.*

*All names are disguised and specific identifying details omitted, a practice followed for all case material in this book.

AN OUTLINE
OF EVENTS

The brief description of work with the Bailey family which follows is intended to give the reader an overall picture of the case before we look at its major phases and then examine the process in detail.

The work lasted for two months with one follow-up session six weeks later. It started when Mr Bailey came to the Area Office of the local Social Services Department, requesting reception into care of his 13-year-old daughter, Mary. He said that he and his wife could no longer cope with Mary, who was staying out late at night and mixing with 'the wrong sort of lads'.

The social workers asked for time to consider this request. With Mr Bailey's permission they assembled information about the family situation from various sources. In addition to what Mr Bailey had told them, there was a closed file in the Department with details about a request for help four years previously, when the parents had been struggling with domestic difficulties that had entailed the wife leaving home for a short period. The education welfare officer (EWO) and the social worker in the neighbourhood team had up-to-date information about the children's educational and social problems. For example, the eldest boy and both girls had poor school attendance.

It was possible at this point to draw up a 'family map'. To the left are the males of the family and to the right the females, with the respective ages of each in brackets beside their names. Important facts about family members are written in the margin. The space in the middle can be used to note how family members relate to each other when this is known.

Figure 2 The Baileys: a family map

manual worker	**Mr Bailey (42)**	**Mrs Bailey (34)**	play-leader (in training)
left school, looking for work	Tony (16)		
		Di (14)	EWO considering court action for non-attendance at school
		Mary (13)	placed at school for maladjusted children, poor attendance; Child Guidance Clinic to reassess; staying out late at night
at school, no known difficulties	Don (12)		
at nursery class, no known difficulties	Jim (3)		

Next an agreement was reached with those agencies concerned with the children's education to suspend their plans and leave the field clear for the Social Services Department to work with the Bailey family for a three months' period. Only then was an offer of help made to the family.

The first interview was concerned with making personal contact with all family members and assessing the current difficulties. An agreement was reached to work with the whole family group for a limited period of time.

The next three interviews (two with the family and one with the couple alone), focused on the family's inability to enjoy life together and their pattern of rows and blaming. The workers gave the family a new experience of having fun together at home by introducing a communication game into the second session. This was much enjoyed, but it became apparent that there was a problem or family secret which the family refused to acknowledge and the level of anger remained very high.

Mary brought matters to a head by breaking into a neighbour's flat and stealing some perfume; she readily admitted her offence. The police obtained a Place of Safety order and placed her in the local assessment centre.

The family workers met with the parents to discuss this crisis. Mr Bailey admitted his own delinquent past, which had been kept a secret from the children until now. He had been imprisoned on a number of occasions, when he was said to be 'working' away from home. Finally when Mrs Bailey had reached the end of her tether four years previously, she had left home. Since that time, Mr Bailey had gone straight. The social workers urged the parents to share this information openly with the family, and acknowledged the parents' courage in facing the truth. Later that day the workers went with Mr and Mrs Bailey to the assessment centre, where Mary was found in good spirits. Mr Bailey and Mary were encourged to talk together and work out an agreement about how to manage their disagreements more constructively. Mr Bailey explained to Mary why he had been strict with her. He wanted to prevent her getting into trouble with the law as he had done. The parents then said that they wanted Mary back home and, following a case conference with the Juvenile Bureau, she was released.

Two days later, in a tense and angry family meeting, Mr Bailey acknowledged and described his imprisonments. The parents were surprised to hear that the children had known the truth all the time. There was angry distressed recollection of the time when Mrs Bailey left home. In this critically important session the family was helped to realize that sharing the truth need not split them apart.

The next two sessions showed a considerable relaxation of tension and an improvement in family relationships. After the central crisis was over, the workers helped family members to consolidate their new ways of relating, without falling back into the 'blaming style' to which they had become accustomed. The needs of the boys in the family were also explored. Plans were made for discussions about Mary's future schooling with the Child Guidance Unit (CGU), and the family was prepared for the termination of the work.

After six weeks a review meeting was held to check out with the family how things were going and to consolidate the progress already made. The atmosphere was much changed – warm and friendly. The difficulties with the children were largely resolved, and the parents were able to praise them for their improved behaviour. Family members were spending more time at home doing things together, and Mr and Mrs Bailey had begun to have weekly nights out on their own for the first time in years. The workers rehearsed with them how they would manage if problems recurred. They said their goodbyes to the family, and advised them to ask for further help if the need should arise in the future.

Later the two girls and the elder boy were encouraged to join evening groups for adolescents. At a case conference at the CGU, in which the workers participated, it was decided to place Mary at a different day school but not to remove her from home.

4 / PHASES OF FAMILY WORK

Any piece of family work may appear too complex to grasp if we try to absorb all its components at once. On the one hand, there is a lot happening in the family, and on the other, the workers may have to make a rapid succession of interventions – which all contribute to the reader receiving a welter of information. In order to ease the reading of the sequence of interventions with its accompanying more technical comments, we shall first discuss the phases through which the work with the Bailey family progressed. Then we will open the curtain fully for the actual events to be seen in the real context of each interview, and discuss the practice issues that they entail.

It would be helpful to say exactly what behaviours family members show at the beginning, the middle, and at the end of a certain family work programme. Unfortunately, we do not have sufficient knowledge yet to specify these fully in very accurate terms. However, on the basis of accumulating experience certain tentative generalizations were made. Experience suggested that, broadly speaking, seven phases seemed to occur in this time-limited piece of family work. These were:

The referral phase
Clearing the field
Induction
Warming up
Approaching the crucial focus
Consolidation
Maintenance and closure.

Only a few comments can be made about each phase within the present space. They did, of course, overlap with each other and some required more sessions than others, but it proved helpful to keep them in mind. Optimally, each follows the other. If a phase is skipped, as for example the 'warming-up' phase tends to be ignored sometimes, the workers and the family may run into unnecessary difficulties later on.

THE REFERRAL PHASE

Usually a family member or a worker of some other agency approaches the social services with a request that they intervene, or 'do something'. It is important to realize that with this step family work itself has already begun. Who approaches the social services, when, and how, are vital pieces of information for future planning. The worker receiving the referral should listen to it with her 'third ear' – find out who is already involved, are they asking for more of the same sort of help they have had for years, why are they asking for help *now*, are there indications that family issues are involved and are we in a position to help?

Careful analysis of the incoming information at the referral stage can save a great deal of trouble later on.

CLEARING THE FIELD

It is important to remember that before family workers make direct contact with the family there are already 'forces' operating in the 'field', such as friends, play groups, schools, or the CGU. These are likely to be sources of influence on the family which may both enhance as well as undermine change. Therefore, before making direct contact with the family it is good to find out who else is involved and whether they are prepared to co-operate with us in a co-ordinated fashion. This sometimes means asking an agency to withhold action for an agreed period of time. It has proved useless to begin working with a family without having sufficient leverage upon the sources that influence it.

INDUCTION

The phase of induction usually takes up the first interview. It also includes the analysis of family behaviours and the selection of foci for intervention by the workers after the first interview. We shall describe this phase in some detail later on. The workers have at least four goals while taking a family through this phase: offering guidelines for communication, decentralizing the index member, observing how family members behave towards each other, and establishing a working relationship and a 'contract' about the work to be undertaken with the family.

WARMING UP

Change cannot be made by families at a stroke; they need to be warmed up to it. Although families may say they want to change, they are often resistant to change and deeply frightened of it. They need to be convinced first, that they can make some changes, however small, which benefit them immediately and second, that the pain required to make changes is not beyond their capacity to absorb it. Therefore, we have to proceed cautiously at first. Out of what the family members have said about their aspirations and according to our observations of how the members have communicated with each other during the first interview, we try to weave in a thread that connects the two. In the second interview we return with a suggestion for a warming-up focus that meets the members' expressed aspirations and sets in motion more effective communication among them. We used the present-giving game in this way with the Baileys. Often the warming-up focus is allocated to the family as a task. Tasks may succeed; they may also fail. It is better that the first task is accomplished. This is easier to secure if the task is performed during the interview. In this way we can be present while the first attempt at change is made. If it runs into difficulties we can help the family immediately.

APPROACHING THE CRUCIAL FOCUS

Once we have warmed up the family to the viability of change, feelings of hope, trust in us, and self-esteem are enhanced. We can then approach issues that entail more pain, yet may bring about more crucial and far-reaching change. Experience suggests that the crucial focus for the family tends to be brought about in two major ways. The first is when we approach it directly; the second is when we begin to remind the family that the programme is to end after three or four more interviews. We call the latter 'countdown'. A direct approach towards the crucial focus can be made when family members express enough of the crucial issue and are at least dimly aware that 'there is something that does not work for us, and this does not make sense'. It is surprising how often countdown may precipitate this too. However approached, the crucial focus usually entails more pain and the members typically present stiffer resistance to change as they struggle through it; their resistance has to be worked through during this stage. It is difficult to predict what proportion of the programme this may take. It may involve working with only parts of the family (children's meetings, couple's session, etc.). It often includes attempts by family members to put the onus on the worker, for example by resorting to material requests, offending, running away from home. Such events can easily cause us to lose sight of the focus of work and to get caught up in the 'drama', particularly so when, due to our statutory responsibilities, there are certain behaviours to which we have to respond. The question is *how* to respond. If the response is such that it is still part of working through the crucial focus, the programme can be enhanced by these crises. In the present case study you will see how we used a crisis that led to the placement of Mary in an assessment centre. We did not allow the 'drama' to side-track us. We knew that Mary and her father had to learn to speak to each other, so this was still our focus while we took the parents to meet Mary at the assessment centre.

CONSOLIDATION

Dramatic, isolated changes of behaviour are not enough if the family is to begin to handle a series of everyday difficulties in a new way. The changes have to be incorporated into the behaviours of all the members. For example, it was not enough to change the relationship between Mary and her father. There were another four siblings in the family. Each of them could then trigger off the old behaviour, no matter how hard Mary and her parents might try to behave differently. Therefore all the family members have to be brought into the work on change and to benefit from it in some way or another. Furthermore, awareness that change could help does not necessarily bring it about. Change has to be experienced as more rewarding than the previous behaviour. A series of 'contracts' can make sure that each member knows what she or he could do to help change and what other members would do on their part. These 'consolidation contracts' have to be worked out in detail with the family, so that they may keep the momentum of change going ahead.

MAINTENANCE AND CLOSURE

The intensive part of the programme usually ends at the consolidation phase. However, life can be full of stormy winds that may all too easily shake loose the newly-acquired behaviours. A follow-up interview is therefore offered to each family four, six, or eight weeks after the end of the programme. If necessary, a second follow-up interview is then arranged after a similar length of time. In between we ask the family to monitor how the new behaviours have been maintained. The new behaviours include reinforcing mutually agreed desirable behaviours among the members. In the follow-up interview these are reviewed and change in them is introduced as and when it is necessary. The way the case is closed is determined by the events that happen during the period of follow-up.

With these phases in mind it will be easier to follow the full 'Bailey story' and to realize that the more technical commentary, added after each interview, stem from other quite diverse frameworks.

5 / THE REFERRAL PHASE

In this chapter we discuss the preparatory work done before the first contact with the family. The work with the Bailey family began on 28 February when the father, Mr Bailey, turned up in reception, at the Area Office of a Social Services Department to ask for his 13-year-old daughter to be received into care. Mr Bailey mentioned that this daughter, Mary, was at a day school for maladjusted children. He said that the family could not cope with her at home anymore. Mary had been staying with neighbours over the weekend. She had been spending too much time out of the flat and was 'mixing with the wrong type of lads'. The parents felt that they had no influence over her. Mr Bailey's concern was acknowledged by the duty social worker, but instead of leaping into action, the worker asked Mr Bailey to give the Department some time to explore how best to help. The duty social worker had a discussion with a colleague in the family workshop, and together they set about exploring the background to the problem. Mr Bailey had given permission to contact other agencies concerned with the family.

It turned out that this family had been offered help by the Office four years previously. Apart from basic information, their file suggested that they had been struggling with serious domestic problems at the time, which led to the wife leaving the home for a few days. The family worker takes over the story as he remembers it:

*   *   *

We felt that the Baileys had shared what was undoubtedly a pressing concern. Indeed we heard that the tenants on the council estate had complained of Di and Mary roaming about with other girls at night. Mary was just over 13 and was young enough to be

exploited. What worried us further was the apparent similarity between the present and the past in this family. It seemed as if whenever the family reached an impasse in their affairs somebody had to be sent out. First it was the mother, and now the daughter, but the 'game' appeared to be similar. With four more children in the family this could develop into what family therapists call a 'game without end' (Watzlawick, Weakland, and Fisch, 1974). Each child could take his/her turn of being sent out (to us, or even worse, to the streets), or a parent would be sent out. Such a repetition of behaviour patterns or recurring problems is what we look for when deciding to offer focused family work. We do this because we accept the view that families go through a series of crises as their members grow up from infancy through childhood to adulthood. The question is how they tackle those crises. Each is different and requires different strategies. 'Going out on' somebody may be an appropriate strategy to resolve conflict during courtship. However, if this strategy is employed in a relationship involving dependent children it is likely to create rather than resolve problems. Whenever the Baileys repeated the 'game' of sending out, they also seemed to need our help. We reflected on whether they had tried any other solutions when under stress. Our records indicated that they had not.

There had been an Education Welfare Officer (EWO) involved. We decided to ask her about the family. We learned from the EWO, Miss Cole, that the eldest son, Tony (now almost 16 years old), had difficulties in attending school in the past. Di, the eldest daughter (almost 15), was going to school so rarely that court action now seemed the only remaining option. Mary herself was placed at a day school for maladjusted children, but rarely attended. The Child Guidance Unit (CGU) was, therefore, reassessing her placement. The two younger boys did not present educational problems. Don (aged 12½ years) was at school, and Jim (aged 3 years) was at a pre-school nursery. However, it seemed that each child might in turn present educational difficulties.

We asked the EWO whether this family had ever been helped as a single unit. The answer was that they were a difficult family and that there had been no resources to offer such a service in the past. The EWO had to deal with each child as and when the difficulties surfaced.

We came to hear more of the family from the senior social worker who was responsible for cases that came to us from the estate on which the Baileys lived. The parents were described as good providers. Mr Bailey, in his early forties, was a self-employed painter and decorator. Mrs Bailey in her mid thirties, was learning to be a play leader. It seemed that they were resourceful people, who had the potential to manage their family affairs; yet the secretary of the Tenants' Association had asked the senior social worker for advice because Di and Mary belonged to a crowd of girls who roamed the estate, disturbing the neighbours and attracting attention from youths too old for them, who might easily exploit them.

It was a puzzling situation. The parents appeared to be good providers and resourceful, but the family relationships kept running into difficulties. Viewed as a system, they repeated the same strategy of one member going out of the family when the going got rough. The children presented serious education and social problems which had been tackled in a piecemeal fashion. Were there enough indicators to encourage us to work with the whole family in a focused way?

The answers that began to emerge with regard to the Baileys were encouraging:

(a) As social workers in a Social Services Department it is our responsibility to help a parent who has requested us to receive his child into care. In view of the other difficulties that the Baileys presented, particularly the fear that Mary and Di would be exploited by older lads, a social work intervention became high priority (see Criterion II p. 41). We discussed the case with the busy senior social worker for the neighbourhood and he sighed with relief when we told him that the Baileys could be offered help from a family worker. It was agreed that with such a large family it would be beneficial for two people to be involved (Oded Manor and a female student).

(b) The fact that it was Mr Bailey who approached us first was encouraging. Often we need to do more work before we know the extent of the father's involvement. There was no doubt about Mr Bailey's concern, or about the active part he played in the family affairs. It was easy to establish that his wife was equally worried. Shared concern makes it easier to convince the parents that everything that happens to one family member affects all the rest. They feel the impact themselves. It is then a smaller step to insist that we meet all who are affected, that is, the whole family (see Criterion III p. 41).

(c) On the face of it, there was no apparent reason why two able adults, like the Bailey couple, could not have more influence over their daughters' behaviour. They were both in touch with their neighbours, knew their locality well, were physically healthy, and able to co-operate to some extent at least with other helping agencies such as the CGU and the schools. Yet most families find an alternative to a situation where one member has to leave. The Baileys seemed unable to do so, which gave us considerable cause for concern (see Criterion IV p. 42).

(d) Having contacted all the other helping agencies that were in touch with the Baileys, it became clear that up to this time nobody had tried to work with them as one group. Help had been offered, particularly by meeting the mother, each time one of the children presented difficulties. Alternating work with one child and the mother is not uncommon. This time we wanted to try to encompass a larger portion of each child's life. Let us take Mary as an example: we wanted to know the ways in which each of the parents handled her; to know more about Di's influence on her; to hear from her school about their view of her; and last but not least, to know what effect Mary's involvement in the girls' crowd had. Indeed, each of the members of the family could be seen as being influenced by a number of 'forces' – the father, mother, siblings, school, or the street. These comprise the member's 'field': their immediate and extended networks. It is often better to effect changes in the whole field, rather than in each part of it in turn (see Criterion V p. 42).

*　　*　　*

□□ **(a) Summary: what the workers did**

1 The workers talked with the duty social worker about Mr Bailey's visit to the office.
2 The workers reviewed the previous contact between the department and the family as recorded in the file.
3 They spoke to the senior social worker in the neighbourhood team who had some information about the family from the people on their estate.
4 They then made contact with the EWO who knew the family.
5 The workers assessed whether the case was appropriate for family work using all the above information.
6 The workers attempted an initial hypothesis about the difficulties that led the family to request help now.

□□ **(b) How else could the situation have been handled?**

Some family workers like to ask the family to come together for an initial discussion *before* reading about past contacts in the file or speaking with professional colleagues. Such workers would rather not pre-judge the issues, and prefer to rely on their own assessment based on observation of the family together and on discussion with family members. However, although there is a good deal to be said for taking a fresh look at a family's problems, it can be a foolhardy undertaking to ignore what is happening in the rest of the family network. Some families attract professional helpers like bees to a honey pot, and it is unproductive to work out a plan of action with the family only to find that this does not fit with an alternative plan already in operation with another agency.

□□ **(c) The referral phase: some basic issues**

PREPARATORY WORK WITH THE CLIENT WHO REFERS A PROBLEM

Very few referrals to social services ask for 'help with a family problem'. Often the request is for a service: a day centre for an elderly person or reception into care of a child. In the latter case the parent of a child in trouble usually comes to the department because of an understanding of its authority and expects prompt action. Even when the problem is not presented in the form of a solution (such as reception into care) the client usually associates the symptom or problematic behaviour with one person only. Mr Bailey came with his request for reception into care; he said that Mary was the problem.

  If the intake worker is exploring whether the case is suitable for family work, there is likely to be a big gap between the worker's perception of her role and the client's perception of it. The client is probably thinking, 'I have come here for social services to do something about this problem'. If family work is to succeed, a conceptual leap is required to a position in which family members are thinking, 'Perhaps if we have help, we can work together to achieve some changes'. The early contacts with the client who refers the problem should be aimed towards helping the family towards the latter view.

It is important to 'start where the client is' but the worker should ask questions which lead gently towards a family perspective: for example, 'What does your wife think about this problem' or 'How do the other children react when X has a tantrum?' If the information given indicates that a number of people within the family are disturbed by the difficulties it will be easier to engage family members in the work.

If the worker is to make a systemic assessment of the family problems, she needs to see the whole family at the first session. The client who refers the problem will usually be reluctant to involve all the others. The client may have previous experience of a setting in which the parent and child are seen alone. A request for the whole family to be seen together can be puzzling. It can also appear vaguely threatening in a family system where one parent normally takes charge, and the other parent is seen as either less capable of working on family problems or unwilling to do so. The client, often the mother, will probably say that her husband refuses to attend, or be reluctant to involve the younger children. Problems about staying off school or work are usually raised. These issues should be fully discussed. (Do people take their children to the dentist during working hours?) The worker should ask the client to talk with her husband again about his willingness to join in a family discussion. In our experience many more fathers are willing to attend than their wives expect. It makes life easier for the family if an appointment can be offered late in the day: between 4 and 7 p.m. for example. The worker should always be clear and firm about her expectations of the family. She can say, 'We think you should all attend. We normally find it helpful and necessary to see members of the family together to understand the problem from different points of view'. Guard against being tentative about this issue. The worker should not take responsibility for the family's problem but *must* take responsibility for the direction of the work.

PREPARATORY WORK WITH A REFERRING AGENT

Frequently a referral is made not by a member of the immediate family, but by another professional worker, or more occasionally by a neighbour or relative. In this case the need for preliminary work before the first family interview is even more essential. The difference in expectations between the family and the worker is likely to be even wider when a third party is acting as go-between.

Occasionally the referring agent has a good knowledge of family work, and what the agency can offer. More frequently there needs to be a period of negotiation in which the worker spells out how the agency can help, and asks the referring agent to discuss with the family a possible plan of action. If the referring agency has given little thought to the referral, or is confused about the functions of the Social Services Department, this period of negotiation may be prolonged. The following example is given to demonstrate how a simple service request turned into a more complex referral for family work.

A GP sent a letter to social services referring Mr Holmes (82) for two weeks respite care in an old people's home, while his wife went on holiday. When a social service aide visited, she found a distressed family. Mr Holmes was bedridden and neglected. He had recently become doubly incontinent and seemed ill. His wife (52) was working fulltime and was strained and resentful of her husband's physical decline. He had worked and been physically active until the age of 75, when he had a minor stroke. The family had not adjusted to that event. The teenage children apparently ignored their father, but were said to be embarrassed by his sudden appearances when they were entertaining friends. The GP had not been asked to visit for some months, and had made the referral after a telephone conversation with the wife, who wanted some relief for herself. The social service aide was concerned that Mr Holmes was ill, and asked the GP to visit. As a result Mr Holmes was admitted to hospital, where he was diagnosed as suffering from heart failure. Later during his convalescence, his family took a holiday. When he returned home Mr Holmes was in better health and no longer incontinent. The case was re-discussed with the GP and a social worker visited the family to assess whether any services could be provided, and also to offer help to the family in adjusting to the father's old age. Both husband and wife were eager to talk about their relationship. The teenage children wished to maintain a distance at first, but were involved at a later stage. Over a period of two months opportunities for help to this family, physical, practical, and emotional, were opened up in a three-way discussion between the GP, the family, and staff of the social services department.

The idea of the referral stage as a three-way negotiation is important. Getting all parties together for a discussion can clarify the issues more quickly than a number of two-way telephone conversations. This idea is developed further in Chapter 6.

ASSESSMENT OF THE INFORMATION

After the first contact with the referring agent, the family worker needs to assess any information available from other sources within the department. If the family has received help before, there will be a file recording previous contacts. A certain amount of information from the records can be useful in making an initial hypothesis about why a problem has arisen. There are some dangers in reading through a 'fat file' loaded with information about a family. One danger is a sense of despair – 'This family is always in trouble. What can I do that will make any difference?' Another danger is that the worker will be over influenced in her judgment about the family, which may after all have changed very considerably since last seen. Unfortunately, few social work files stress the strengths and abilities of family members. Other sources may know facts about the family which round out the picture of them. For example, it was the senior social worker in the neighbourhood team who could tell the family workers about the Baileys' areas of competence.

CRITERIA FOR OFFERING FAMILY WORK

When basic information about the family and its problems has been assembled, the intake worker will decide how to allocate the case. If the problem is obviously one of family relationships or disturbing behaviour in a child, family work should be considered as an option.

A great deal of research needs to be done before we can state with any certainty which criteria for the selection of what method of work are sound (Walrond-Skinner 1976). The following criteria are those we have used for deciding whether a case is appropriate for family work.

(I) Is the client currently part of a family group?
(II) Is the problem within the terms of reference of the agency?
(III) Do members of the family (particularly the parents) share a concern about the problem?
(IV) Is there any indication that family members could handle things differently?
(V) Has family work been offered to the family before, and if so, to what effect?
(VI) Are the family workers ready to tackle all the levels of difficulty of the work?

(I) *Is the client currently part of a family group?*

If the client is single and separated from his family, he is more likely to be preoccupied with his development as an individual, and individual work will be the method of choice. Even here a family perspective is important: the themes, myths, and experiences from our primary family follow us throughout life.

Some social workers believe that adolescents should be offered individual work, on the grounds that they need help with problems of identity, and with their movement towards independence from the family. Our view is that some adolescents will be unable to leave the family until the family system frees them to do so. We have found that a combination of family work, plus a group for the adolescent, is helpful for families at that life stage.

(II) *Is the problem within the terms of reference of the agency?*

The Social Services Department has very wide terms of reference, but that does not mean that it should (or can) take on all comers. All departments should be clear about what referrals should *not* be accepted, and should have a clear order of priority for work undertaken. For example, if the problem is truancy, the Education Welfare service will clearly be better placed to deal with it, as the EWO has access to both the key systems involved with the child – school and family.

(III) *Do members of the family share a concern about the problem?*

We need to explore how the presenting problem affects others in the family. Sometimes everyone is distressed, and the problem is clearly a 'family concern'. This is often the case when someone in the family has been diagnosed as mentally ill: the patient may be acutely unhappy, confused, or withdrawn, or doing bizarre or frightening things; others in the family will be accommodating themselves to this 'sick' behaviour continually. They may say, 'We can never leave him alone'. They will be feeling considerable pressure or distress themselves, and may be motivated to join in discussions about how to cope with the problem.

On other occasions, the problem will impinge less on the family. If a child of fifteen is truanting, and his parents had a poor experience of school themselves and believe that their child should be out at work, the level of anxiety within the family will be low. Although all members of the family will have an opinion about the truancy, which may be helpful in preparing a social enquiry report, there are contra-indications for on-going family work.

(IV) *Is there any indication that members of this family could handle things differently?*

This is an invitation to consider the family's strengths and history of managing past conflicts. Too often assessments are dominated by family pathology. Social work is so problem-centred and clients so often seen at a time of stress or weakness, that it is easy to underestimate their strengths. The parents may have important skills and relationships in the work setting; they may manage their finances well; and have a pleasant home. The children may be acceptable within their peer group, may be good at music or football. Even dysfunctional behaviour can be associated with positive qualities: a boy who is in trouble for stealing scrap iron may be exploratory and daring; a school-phobic child may be sensitive and imaginative. An exploration of strengths at the referral stage begins marginally to alter the family's view of itself, and its ability to handle things better.

It is also important to ask how the family has managed past difficulties. The Baileys fell back on 'sending someone out of the family' when they reached an impasse in family life. Themes, such as excluding someone, are often found in family life. Other families have managed previous life transitions successfully, but have come up against a serious crisis all of a sudden. It is then important to ask, 'Why now . . . ?'

(V) *Has family work been offered to this family before, and if so, to what effect?*

Very often (as in the case of the Baileys), family members have not been seen together for previous help. It was common in the past to exclude the father in casework. Throughout society there is now a greater expectation of help from fathers, who are allowed to participate in the birth of their own children, and are more likely to help in their upbringing. Often the father is glad to be asked to participate, and it is absolutely essential that he should.

Siblings, even when they are less involved, may be acute observers of family process, and can be useful in uncovering areas of family conflict which would otherwise be unmentionable.

If family work has been tried before, without success, this is generally a contra-indication; but there are reasons why it may have failed apart from the unresponsiveness of the family: it might have been that the worker lacked experience.

(VI) *Are the family workers ready to tackle all levels of difficulty in family work?*

Sometimes in the early stages of learning to work with families it may be sensible to exclude certain types of problem at the referral stage, on the grounds of difficulty: an example might be a case where there has been non-accidental injury to a child.

RESPONDING TO A REQUEST FOR HELP: ORGANIZATION

The intake system in a social work agency can be more responsive to the needs of the organization than to the needs of the client. Carole Addison (1982) in a paper about intake in a Social Services Department, suggests that this is due to the disabling level of anxiety carried by intake workers who are faced by a quantity and variety of work that is formidable; work that is more often than not of a serious and worrying nature. Many social workers dread periods on duty and feel 'under siege' by the public. Addison draws on Isobel Menzies' ideas (1970) about institutional defenses to suggest that social services staff have developed attitudes and work procedures that help them to avoid the full impact of public needs. These defensive practices range from barriers to access (such as limited telephone facilities, unclear notices, and poor reception), to intake practices which enable staff to avoid the full emotional impact of contact with suffering individuals. For example, the duty rota may be organized so that the same client is rarely seen by the same social worker twice.

Addison suggests the following ways in which intake systems can be made more responsive to the public:

(a) a study of intake practices to raise consciousness among staff;
(b) recognition by management of the high level of anxiety among workers who have contact with the public; and
(c) planning to deal with this anxiety in a more rational way through (for example) better support systems for staff, and the setting of realistic objectives in the work.

It is hard to set up a good intake system for family work which is unrelated to an attempt to improve the overall system. Such an attempt is hard to undertake in a period of recession, when pressure on staff is particularly heavy. Perhaps it is important to say that rationing of services is inevitable; demand can never be fully met. The issue is whether more can be done by social workers with less anxiety if the system is organized in a rational way. We are conscious that many workers suffer from considerable secondary anxiety about the poor practice which flows from an over-defended system.

Let us assume that a serious attempt is being made by intake workers to respond to requests for help at the right time, and in a manner likely to make an open negotiation about the help needed a possibility. In these circumstances, we would take the view that the assessment discussion about a family problem should take place between the client (or referring agent) and a family worker. The worker with a systemic orientation will be more successful in engaging a family group than an intake worker who normally works with individual clients. When a client first comes to the office, or when a telephone referral is first taken, it is usually possible to obtain enough facts to know whether family work should be considered. An early appointment with a family worker should be made then and there for an assessment discussion with the client. (An alternative strategy would be to train intake workers to deal with the assessment stage in family work.)

The problem of organization is how to make a few family workers easily available for assessment interviews. Intake systems are organized in diverse ways, and it is not possible for us to prescribe how the problem should be solved. We can only offer suggestions from our own practice. For example:

(a) members of intake teams who are trained in family work can act as 'guardians'; they take responsibility for selecting and assessing family cases;
(b) a senior family worker can
   – check all referrals that come into duty and select those which may be suitable for family work;
   – act as a consultant to those who may need advice about a particular case at the referral stage;
   – provide a regular weekly time on duty (preferably in the early evening) for assessment interviews; these can also be done on a rota basis by a number of workers.

With thought and determination to provide a good service from the start, it is possible to use whatever intake structure you have to reach families at the right time and in the right way. We shall present some examples from our own practice in the second part of Chapter 13.

RESPONDING TO A REQUEST FOR HELP: TIMING

Beyond the organizational constraints there are factors that stem from the dynamics of reactions to any crisis. Individual family members ask for help in crisis, but there seems to be a variation in the time at which they are receptive to therapeutic intervention. At the referral stage we are normally dealing with one individual from the family group; we are attempting to engage that individual in the process of bringing the family together. It is important to understand the likely impact of changes on that person. The study by Adams, Hayes, and Hopson (1976) of individual behaviour during periods of transition indicates that, whatever the type of transition, the cycle of reactions and feelings is predictable. They identify seven stages:

1 *Immobilization* – the individual feels overwhelmed by the process of change, is unable to plan.
2 *Minimization of the change* – defenses such as denial are used to give time for adjustment.
3 *Depression* – is likely as the need for change begins to be acknowledged.
4 *Acceptance of the new reality* – the individual 'lets go' of the past, feels new optimism.

5 *Testing out* – new behaviours are tried in relation to the changed situation; there is a high level of energy, also irritation/anger.

6 *Seeking meanings* – there is an attempt to understand the change in circumstances and relationships, and the ambivalence about it.

7 *Internalization of the meaning* – the changed attitudes and feelings become part of the person.

Our hypothesis, based on casework experience rather than on research, is that the later in this period of transition an individual refers himself or his family the more likely it is that he will be receptive to an offer of family work. At stage 1 the client who is asking for help will be immobilized and unable to plan, though probably grateful for the chance to share his anxieties. At stage 2 he temporarily lowers his anxiety by the use of powerful defenses, such as projection or denial. He blames 'outsiders' such as school, or separates himself from the family problem by indicating that another family member is 'bad' or 'sick'. If referred by another agency, he may deny the seriousness of the problems. However, once the client begins to acknowledge a need for changes which include himself (stage 3) there is some chance of a contract for family work being negotiated. As self-esteem increases and the energy level rises (stages 4–6) so does the chance of a successful negotiation.

This hypothesis appears to be supported by some research at the Institute of Marital Studies (IMS) (Daniell 1981) based on interviews with twenty-two wives and husbands. A feature common to all these couples was the time lag between the onset of their problems and their request for help:

'At the point of coming to the IMS many couples appeared to have reached the later phases of the transition process, where a shift had occurred and the focus was on struggling to understand the particular meaning of the change . . . . It was only in the later phases that they were able to become more aware of, and *responsible for*, their re-adjustment to a new state, both within their inner, intra-physic world, and within their relationships.' (Our emphasis)   (Daniell 1981)

The implication of these ideas is that if a client refers himself or his family at an early stage in the change process, it is important to hold him through the early phases until he reaches a state of mind in which he can negotiate for help, rather than asking to have the problem removed by an outsider.

☐☐ (d) A case example related to timing: 'The twitch on the thread'

This case illustrates our hypothesis that family members should be allowed to carry their own anxiety till ready to move towards a change.

The Linden family had reached a difficult transition in family life. A year earlier, Mr and Mrs Linden, both with good work records, had been made redundant within a month of each other, and had been unable to find work since. The inevitable stress of unemployment and a severely reduced income had engendered marital conflict. This was exacerbated by two important events in the development of the children. The eldest, Keith, a son from Mr Linden's first marriage, had become engaged, and was talking of leaving home. This event drew Mr Linden's mind back to the unsuccessful early marriage upon which he had entered as a youth of the same age as his son. Mrs Linden was made anxious by the thought of her chief ally, Keith, leaving the family. The parents' anxiety was raised further by the adolescent behaviour of their daughter, Diana. A precocious 12-year-old, Diana had reached the age at which Mrs Linden herself had been received into care after her parents' marriage broke up. Because of their earlier experiences, Mr and Mrs Linden were terrified of the conflict which occasionally erupted between them. Diana, ultra-sensitive to her parents' feelings, would endeavour to stop the rows whenever they happened, and increasingly drew attention to herself through rebellious behaviour.

These facts became clear during an assessment interview with a family worker, which took place after Mrs Linden requested Diana's reception into care. Help was offered to the family as a group, but the parents did not commit themselves to the task of family change until six months later. During that time, Diana remained a serious problem to her parents. She was truanting from school and staying out at night. On two occasions she ran away from home, and was found by the police in a bed and breakfast hotel, staying with an 18-year-old girlfriend. The parents were unwilling to take action together to control her: in some ways mother was over-involved, but her constant nagging had become ineffective, and she was inconsistent in her messages to her daughter; father was unwilling to take a firm line himself, but often undermined his wife when she spoke harshly to Diana. Mother blamed the school, the police, social services, Diana's friends, and Diana herself. Father completely denied the seriousness of the problems. This high level of defensiveness in the parents – projection by Mrs Linden and denial by Mr Linden – originated in the painful earlier events in their own lives. They maintained these defences (stage 2) for over six months, when they began to move forward through the transition, and acknowledged, in a depressed way (stage 3), their own part in the difficulties. During a six months' hiatus, although refusing help for the family group, Mrs Linden asked for Diana to be received into care several times. The school and the EWO also wanted some action to be taken by the local authority. Meanwhile the parents were offered alternative help at the Child Guidance clinic, but failed to keep the appointments. The family worker who had interviewed the family in the first place remained convinced that this family had considerable strengths and could deal with their own problems if they would only take the plunge, and moreover that it would resolve nothing to receive Diana into care. The family worker took responsibility for monitoring information about the family, responding to anxious queries by other departments with the statement, 'We have made an offer of help to this family and that remains open. We believe that this family has the capacity to work on this problem if they choose to do so'. On three occasions of crisis during the six months' hiatus period, the social worker wrote to Mr and Mrs Linden restating the offer of help to the family. Finally the parents reached the moment when they were prepared to move: family sessions started. The situation had deteriorated so far that Diana needed a short period in an assessment centre in order to give her a clear message about adult control, but it was not necessary to institute care proceedings, and she returned home after six weeks. The family probably moved from stage 2 of minimization to stage 4 of accepting that something new had to happen.

After a period of regular family sessions, the parents' management of Diana changed considerably. She began behaving like a 12-year-old, and the Education Authority found a place for her at a different school, where she did well. The parents began to communicate better between themselves, and to acknowledge their differences more openly, and with less fear. There was no recurrence of problems six months later. In this case the family worker gave a 'twitch on the thread' from time to time. The parents were given a clear and consistent message, and in the end they were ready to act for themselves, rather than wanting the problem (and the child) taken away. We believe that this sort of approach should be taken more often by local authority social workers. The timing of an offer of help is obviously important, and the family may not be ready on the first occasion that they present a crisis.

It is possible that some readers are feeling that it was irresponsible of the social worker to leave Diana in the community at risk for six months, rather than taking responsibility for her through a reception into care. We are of the opinion that the risks remain for children in care who are linked into their family system in a destructive way; readers will remember many children who continue to act out after reception into care, running back to their families or their peer group, or bringing their challenges and their violence into a children's home. Sometimes a child is freed from family pressure by reception into care, but then all too often, siblings take over the role of scapegoat within the family, and one by one the children follow each other into care like beads on a string. If a worker feels that a family should not be relieved of immediate stress through a reception into care (or any other 'rescue' measure which temporarily removes the problem from the family), there should be full discussions with those managers ultimately responsible for the work. A clear case must be made for the decision not to intervene, indicating (a) how family pressures appear to be contributing to the child's behaviour and (b) what evidence the social worker has for assuming that the family is capable of change, given time.

□□ (e) Activities for further learning – *the suggestions below are intended to give you practice in working with clients at the referral stage:*

1 Role-play a discussion between a client and a family worker who is offering an appointment to the family group.
2 Take two recent referrals of family problems to your agency. Look at the process of negotiation between the intake worker and the client; think what helped and what hindered that negotiation.
3 Discuss your intake system and plan how to obtain suitable family referrals.

6 / CLEARING
THE FIELD

This chapter begins with the workers' account of further activities undertaken before approaching the Bailey family.

*   *   *

Having established the Baileys' suitability for focused family work, we now attempted to gain some control over their common 'field'. We needed to establish a certain amount of control if we were to influence the forces in it. Some forces were beyond our reach at first and we needed to discuss the situation fully with the family before initiating direct action. We could not contact the girls' crowd yet but we made contingency plans. For instance, we established with our Intermediate Treatment Centre (ITC) their ability and wish to offer the girls the use of their premises. This should offer far more constructive, not to mention safer, ways for the girls to spend their time. Miss Cole, the EWO, knew how we worked from our co-operation with her in the past. We explained our plan to her. We asked for her office to delay court action with regard to Di's non-attendance at school until we completed our programme with the Baileys (providing that this proved acceptable to them). Miss Cole agreed and, at her request, we put our plan in writing for her supervisor's consideration. The supervisor allocated us the three months we asked for before she would act. We negotiated with the CGU in the same way. They too were willing to postpone reassessment of Mary's placement for three months. We, on our part, said to both agencies that we would be briefing them continously about the course of our work with the Baileys. Particularly, we asked Miss Cole to keep in close touch because she knew Di and Mary well. Later on, one of the most critical stages of our work with the Baileys was immensely helped through one of her intelligent and sensitive interventions.

*   *   *

□□ **(a) Summary: what the workers did**

The workers cleared the field before approaching the family by:

1 Gathering information from the existing office records of previous work with the family.
2 Gathering information from the education welfare office (EWO) involved.
3 Gathering information from the senior social worker of the social services team involved.
4 Convincing the senior EWO to allow them three months of working with the family before the EWO took any action.
5 Convincing the CGU to allow them three months of working with the family before the Unit proceeded with their reassessment.
6 Assuring all agencies involved that they would be receiving information about the progress of work with the family.
7 In particular, forming close links with the EWO already involved and making contingency plans with her.

□□ **(b) How else could the situation have been handled?**

The workers could have asked the senior social worker to convene a case conference. He would then have had to invite the senior EWO and the EWO involved, a representative from the CGU and the youth worker in that neighbourhood. Such a meeting would have ensured not only that each worker had clarified her plan but equally that each of them knew the others' plans. This would have increased the co-operation among all concerned.

□□ **(c) Clearing the field: some basic issues**

Many workers complain that their work with families is undermined by the interventions of other agencies. This may be true. However, in our experience, others are more likely to intervene when you have adopted a siege mentality: workers sometimes behave as if they are trapped in a besieged castle. They assume in advance that others are there only to disrupt their work and are very likely to do just the wrong thing. This siege mentality is destructive; it is also totally alien to a systemic approach which says that we are all in a web of systems and sub-systems in need of contact with each other if change is ever to occur. Therefore, the first question that the family worker asks is not, 'Who may interrupt me?' but, 'Who is already included in the system?' The system includes formal sub-systems such as the EWO or the hospital, as well as informal ones, for instance members of a club to which an adult goes, or some part of the extended family (grandparent, uncle, friends, etc.).

The second question is 'Who already has the power in this system and over what issues?' For example it may turn out that a club to which a family member goes exerts more influence on that person than anybody in the family; or that a family member is seeing a psychiatrist at the hospital who has already established some major influence

on him. In that case, the worker should liaise with those who have the influence. If she does not the family member will contact his old resource just when the whole system faces the need to change. He will then come back and say for example 'I saw my doctor yesterday and he said . . . '. It is quite likely that more often than not, the family member will have contrived to elicit a message which aims at stabilizing the previous state of affairs. Homeostasis, the family's steady state which militates against change, will thus be strengthened. We call such action 'activating Dr Homeostat'. The only way to avoid the opposition of 'Dr Homeostat' is to include him in your work right from the start. This can often be done if *before* you offer the contract to the family you gather the whole system and negotiate who is going to be involved and in what way. The best approach is to develop an overall system view with all concerned and arrive at a shared understanding of who is in the best position to do what. You can introduce this by saying something like 'Since each of you has already done good work with one part of the family, I wonder if it is now the time to try and put it all together by meeting them as a group'. It may well become self-evident that a worker who has not been involved with any part of the family is in the best position to initiate such a move and you will obtain the permission you need.

It is always important to acknowledge the other workers' perspectives and efforts. Every discipline has its own set of assumptions: Child Guidance workers are often influenced by psychodynamic thinking; EWO are especially in tune with educational concepts. The point is to weave your systemic ideas into their constructs of the child's needs. You may be able to 'translate' a girl's need to compete with her mother (a psychodynamic concept) to a parallel of her relationship with her female teacher (an educational perspective), while pointing out that all this may well have to do with the way father exerts his power in the family (a more 'law and order' orientation). By showing how each of the other workers' perspectives contributes towards the whole picture the worker validates what everybody has already done. Instead of appearing to claim that it is the family worker who has the solution, she may say that the other workers' interventions are clearly logical (which they usually are) and she is not sure that anything she may try will be better (which is the honest stance to take before one has tried to do the work). Putting ideas across tentatively may help avoid defensiveness and counter-criticism from others.

© T Benjamin

In short, having harnessed the system . . .

Of course, any worker may at times fail to arrive at an agreement with other agencies. If in the end it is clear that the worker is not given sufficient power by those already involved, it is better to say so and hand over the case. The worker may say something like 'In view of our discussion it seems that you (a particular colleague) already know the family very well and have established a good relationship with them. Since for me to be of any help to them I should need to deal with the whole situation for a while, it may be better that you do it and I shall offer you whatever help you think is useful.' It is surprising how often people give others the power they need once there is no competition over it.

If in the end all the other workers agree that the family worker will work with the family for a period of time, that worker should not imagine that they are then out of it. The family members will have to be told of contacts and agreements with other agencies. With the family's permission, the worker will have to continue to keep the other agencies in the picture. They do not usually need to know the details but an overall knowledge of how the work is progressing, and what results may be expected at each stage is helpful to them. Once they know this, very few will feel the need to interrupt. In short, having harnessed the system, it must be fed. If the system is not fed with the appropriate information throughout the work, somebody in it will interrupt at the moment when it is most difficult to cope with any interference.

□□ (d) A different example related to clearing the field: the Ingram family

The Ingram family reached the Social Services Department first through the juvenile court. Their daughter, Sally, was taken to court by the EWO because she had not attended school for a long time. The EWO described the parents as highly co-operative and was at a loss to understand Sally's non-attendance.

An Interim Care Order was granted by the court for twenty-eight days in order to enable the local assessment centre to form an opinion about Sally. Sally would not say anything beyond answering 'yes' or 'no'. Since the case was also brought for allocation to the appropriate social service team, the social services workers began to harness the system by joining forces with the staff of the assessment centre. The social worker in charge of the centre joined the field family worker in working with the Ingrams. Furthermore, consultation immediately began with the EWO, the educational psychologist and the psychiatrist. They told the workers that there was no objective reason for Sally to be out of school. The information that the psychiatrist was able to pick up suggested possible sources of distress at home. In view of this, the workers offered the Ingrams a home visit and asked the whole family to be there. What they saw and heard at home more than convinced them of the possibility that Sally was signalling an important message about her family situation. Since some of it was recognized by the family (continuous and intense rows between Sally and her sisters), the workers felt able to go back to the court and, with the family's approval, ask for the case to be adjourned for a period of four months. It was explained that an agreement had been made with the family to use that time to meet together and work on a resolution of Sally's difficulties at home. It seemed quite clear that the support offered by all the other professionals was vital in convincing the court to accept it.

□□ (e) Activities for further learning

These exercises are better shared among three workers.

1 Go over cases each of you has handled and check with each other to what extent you 'harnessed the system' *and* continued to 'feed it'.

2 Go over those cases again and hypothesize: what would have been the effects of agreeing to a time-limit for each piece of work in advance as far as other agencies' behaviour was concerned?

3 Divide into 'family worker', a 'worker from another agency' and 'an observer'. In a comfortable room the 'family worker' and the 'other worker' should face each other while the 'observer' sits so that she can see both. Begin a role-play where the family worker's task is to *initiate* a dialogue with the other worker (perhaps a CGU social worker) about offering family work to a family both workers know. The observer's task is to monitor:

   – Does the family worker really initiate a dialogue? If so, How?
   – Is the family worker able to get into the other worker's shoes or does she impose her ideas? How?
   – Is there a hidden agenda growing between the parties or a power struggle building up unacknowledged? How?

After ten minutes of role-play the observer should give feedback to both parties, and the episode should be discussed by all.
Then change roles and role-play another episode in the same way, giving each of you an opportunity to play each of the roles.

7 / INDUCTION

This chapter describes the first direct contact with the family. Usually it happens during the first session and with the whole family. The first session sets the scene for the rest and is, therefore, crucial for what is to follow. For this reason, we examine it in detail here, but let us first turn to the workers' account of that session with the Baileys.

*   *   *

We had prepared the wider field of the Bailey family as carefully as possible prior to our intervention. It was time to approach them directly. We sent the family a letter. In it we explained that we wanted to meet with all of them about six times at their home. We insisted that they were all there because 'everything that happened to one of them affected all the rest', and we needed to hear what each member had to say, 'Yes, including little Jim'. The parents telephoned to accept our offer of a family interview.

13 March

First family interview: INDUCTION – *engaging the family and assessing their behaviour*

ARRIVAL

We took care to arrive at the Baileys on time. Tony opened the door for us and quickly directed us to the living room where the whole family had already gathered. This looked like a good sign. They seemed to be expecting us. However, none of them would introduce themselves to us.

INDUCTION

Focused family work is active and direct. We took the initiative, introduced ourselves and asked all the family members to do likewise. In a light and brief manner we then explained clearly how it came about that we were there, why we wanted the family to meet together and what we intended to offer. The family members listened with little comment.

DRAWING OUT STRENGTHS

We continued to offer leadership by first eliciting the family's strengths. To make it meaningful to the Baileys we said that before we could find out how their situation could be improved it would be better to get to know each other a little. Particularly, we said, it would be nice to know what each of them liked to do in their spare time. This tactic seemed to take them by surprise. It may well have shaken their preconceived expectations further when one of us expressed our enjoyment of music. Family members tended to cringe a little, as if embarrassed. Such signs of embarrassment during the first moments may have been associated with the fact that we were not perceived as interested in what was 'bad' in the family. Instead, we were first showing interest in what was 'good'. We were also signalling that there were strengths in the family and possibilities for enjoyment and that these were important to us. We still kept the initiative when going round the room asking the members about their hobbies, yet it became apparent that conversation in the Bailey family was channelled through the mother. Whenever somebody was hesitant she was always the first to help. We respected her role at this stage, and did not interrupt her, let alone comment on her behaviour (Haley 1976: 21–7). However, we did suggest that each member should try to speak for him or herself.

REPHRASING

When the round was finished we checked directly with the individual members of the family that we had understood each of their interests correctly — for example, 'so you, Don, like woodwork and football, and you, Mary, like going to the disco', etc. This shows the family the positive and validating effect that direct speech has and that we have tried to listen. It also helps us to sharpen our memory.

DRAWING OUT TARGETS FOR CHANGE

With the reins still in our hands, we then approached areas of possible change while all the time leaving gaps for spontaneous behaviour by the members, and observing them closely. We now asked each of them what they would like to be 'made better' in their family. Taking this step is often like walking across a mine-field. Various members will try to draw the workers' attention to their concern only. The difficulty that brought the family to us is a natural trap. It takes some skill to adequately acknowledge the value of all that is being expressed whilst explaining that discussion of some topics will have to be postponed until later. One of us recalled a teacher's dictum, 'when in doubt, move about', which proved to be useful. We needed to show we were attending to the points that were being made by each family member, yet to keep the momentum going. The Baileys tended to side-track us with mutual accusations about each other's inaccuracies, with arguments and depreciative comments directed towards each other. The atmosphere certainly warmed up and it was our turn to feel embarrassed. It felt as if the Baileys were now on their home ground. The language of accusations and quarrels sounded well oiled.

REPHRASING AGAIN

We controlled the heat by again going round and asking for specific descriptions only. When everybody had had their say we checked with each of them that we had got their messages right.

CONCLUDING AND ESTABLISHING A CONTRACT

We then said that a great deal had been expressed already and that we wanted to conclude the meeting at this point so that we could have time to think about it all. We engaged the family in contracting again the agreement to have six family sessions. We said that we felt we had got to know the family a little now, that there seemed to be plenty of liveliness in it, and that the difficulties had become clearer too. We thought that it was worthwhile to work towards resolving them, but that this would be hard work and at times painful. We offered to meet with the whole family the following week. We checked with the parents and each child whether they were willing to do this. All family members consented to such a meeting.

*　　*　　*

□□ **(a) Summary: what the workers did**

1 Prior to the first session of their work with the Bailey family, the workers had decided how to approach the family directly – by letter – and had planned the session.
2 During the first session, the workers set out rules for effective communication and started to teach these to the family.
3 They engaged each member of the family by approaching them directly during the session. This served two functions, first it reinforced the message that each family member is equally important. Second, the effect was to take some of the pressure off the index member or 'scapegoat', in this case Mary. This process is known as 'decentralizing the index member' and will be discussed later.
4 The workers elicited each person's strengths, so the family could see themselves

and each other as people with good qualities and not just problems. **This is particularly important for the index member.**

5 **Throughout the session the workers were observing the process of interaction, so they were able to assess both the strengths in the family, and how they dealt with difficulties.**

6 **The workers then moved on to enabling the family to identify targets for change.**

7 **Having done this, they made an agreement with the whole family to work together towards these aims for an agreed number of sessions. The setting up of a mutual agreement between the family and the workers about the purpose and duration of their work together is known as a contract.**

□□ (b) How else could the situation have been handled?

The workers' format for Induction is only one among many. It is, more than anything else, an application of Satir's ideas (Satir 1967), where communication and strengths are taken up with the family right from the start. It should be stressed that there are, of course, other styles, notably Minuchin's way of first 'joining' the family, before 'unbalancing' its equilibrium later on (Minuchin 1974), and Haley's carefully paced build-up of trust, the presentation of the problem, interaction among family members, and the definition of the desired change (Haley 1976). There clearly is so much to learn about the beginning of family work (Stierlin *et al.* 1980; Teismann 1980), that we cannot even begin to cover it here.

□□ (c) Induction: some basic rules

BEFORE THE SESSION

First Contact

The workers need to decide how to contact the family. The obvious choices are by telephone or letter. The telephone has the advantage of being quick, and enabling a response. The major disadvantage is that it is not possible to address each family member equally by telephone and there is no guarantee that what is said on the telephone to one family member will be transmitted accurately to the others. Also, if the telephone is used the risk is that the workers give the family different messages at the same time. One message is that the workers wish to meet all the members of the family together, yet on the telephone only one family member is addressed directly. If the family have had previous contact with the agency, and already have expectations of the response they will get, it may be difficult to modify that if the worker's initial reaction is the same as previously. There is also a risk that the worker may unknowingly collude with one family member.

For example, the Driver family were referred because of difficulties with their teenage son, who had been in trouble with the police. Mrs Driver had asked for help from the Social Services Department on several previous occasions, and the help offered had involved her and her son. Her husband had not been invited to participate. At the point of the new referral, the workers' aim was to involve the whole family, and particularly Mr Driver, in the discussions. The choice of first contact was between speaking to Mrs Driver on the phone since her husband was out at work all day, or writing to the family. The workers chose to write to Mr and Mrs Driver, Michael and Sarah, his sister, to ensure that Mr Driver was given the message from the first contact that his involvement was vital. They were aware that had their first contact been with Mrs Driver on the telephone, the workers might have jeopardized the chance of involving Mr Driver too.

When using a letter in a statutory social work agency, it is useful to include the following points:

(i) Ensure that the letter is written to each family member by name, regardless of their age. For example: 'Dear Mr and Mrs Driver, Michael and Sarah'.

(ii) Point out that each family member is expected to participate. The underlying assumption is that what happens to one member of the family affects all the others and that the workers value each person's contribution. This is an acknowledgement of the view of the family as a system.

(iii) Explain that the contact will be time limited – usually between six and twelve sessions.

(iv) Explain that the work will involve trying to help the family improve their situation. The family will probably have expectations that the workers will want to hear about all their difficulties, especially if they have had contact with the Social Services Department previously. It is useful to establish that the workers are hoping to enable the family to change the situation for the better themselves. This gives them the message that the workers will try to make it safer for them to change, but that the responsibility for the change remains with the family.

(v) Ask the family to ensure that everybody reads and/or understands the letter. This is particularly relevant in families with severe communication difficulties, that is where people are not speaking to each other, and/or where the family members may have varying degrees of literacy.

(vi) The workers need to decide whether the session will be in the office or at the family's home. The obvious advantage of visiting the family at home is to enable the workers to gain information by seeing them in their own environment. This may also be appropriate if the family have an elderly or handicapped member, or for other practical reasons. The major advantage of having sessions in the office is that it is easier for the workers to take charge of the session. This is true in physical terms, for example the workers can set the right number of chairs in position. Also it is unlikely that there will be as many interruptions in the office environment. It is much more difficult to ask the family to move their chairs so that they can see each other easily, or to turn the television off when they are in their own home! It is also important if the worker wants to build up confidence in taking the initiative in work, as it is likely that the workers will feel more comfortable on their own ground.

An example of a letter

Dear Mr and Mrs Driver, Michael and Sarah

We understand that Michael has recently been in trouble with the police and is due to appear in Court on 12 May. We understand that you would like to discuss this situation with a Social Worker.

We are Social Workers who work with the whole family together and we would like to meet with all of you. You can each raise any issues you wish as we think it is important to hear everybody's point of view.

You may decide at our first meeting that it would be helpful for us to work together for a short time to try and make your situation better. In that case, we usually offer six or eight sessions on a fortnightly basis.

We would be glad if you will come to the office at 6 p.m. on Tuesday, 7 April. If this is inconvenient for any one of you, please let us know and we will arrange another time. Otherwise we will look forward to meeting you all then.

Would you please make sure that everybody in the family sees this letter.

Yours sincerely

Jane Thomas
Anne Horton
Social Workers

It is often helpful to enclose a stamped addressed envelope for the family to reply.

PLANNING THE SESSION

Time will need to be spent with your co-worker before the first session (as indeed every session) in planning, usually in consultation with the supervisor and/or support group. The main aim of the first session is to engage the family, and to gather information, not to start change. In order to do this, the worker will be taking initiatives during the session which will increase the involvement of the family (Haley 1976). The first task is to identify the steps of this session in detail.

A plan for a first session could be

  (i)   Introductions – introduce yourselves to each member of the family directly, refer to the letter, clarify why you are there.
  (ii) Ask each family member something about themselves; for example what they enjoy doing. This is to elicit their strengths, and observe how they relate to each other around positive experiences.
  (iii) Summarize what each family member has said, and make links between their contributions where possible.
  (iv) Ask each family member what they would like changed for the better in the

family. Some family members will refer to the presenting problem, but others may mention quite separate issues, for example, going out more together. In this way members' aspirations are identified and their behaviour around areas of concern can be observed.

(v) Summarize and link again (as in iii).

(vi) Make the contract. This will involve:

> – The family's commitment to the work. Agreement must be reached about who will attend the sessions.
> – The issues to be worked on (write down if possible).
> – Number of sessions; negotiate time, and frequency.

Having done this, the workers can then plan how each part of the session will be handled. If there are two workers, it can be useful for one worker to have the main responsibility for each part of the session. This reduces any confusion between the workers, and each knows when to help if, or when, their partner gets 'stuck'!

It is useful to think in advance of the situations that the workers may face when they get to the session, and of the points that need special attention when deciding what each will do.

. . . each knows when to help if, or when, their partner gets 'stuck'!

□□ (d) Crucial issues during the first session

THE MINIMUM SUFFICIENT NETWORK

It is important to decide which family members the workers feel must be present, in order to do any effective work; or whether work can start without one or more of them (Skynner 1971).

In our earlier example, Mr Driver did not arrive for the first session. The workers had agreed in advance that his involvement was vital in order for any effective change to take place in the family. They had agreed they must stick to their original message to Mr Driver that he was important, and that they did value his contribution. They also suspected that, in view of the family's previous experience of the Social Services Department, Mr Driver would be reluctant to trust them, and presume that they were more likely to listen to his wife's point of view than his. For these reasons, the workers did not hold a session. They negotiated another time that would be convenient with Mrs Driver, Michael and Sarah, explaining that it was so important to have Mr Driver there that they could not start without him. Mrs Driver offered to make sure he came next time, and the workers said they would write to him with the new appointment. Mr Driver not only attended the next session, but had arranged to leave work early in order to ensure that the rest of the family were ready in time!

The first session is crucial to the whole piece of work with the family. Experience shows that it is worth insisting on everybody being present, whatever their age, in order to gain as much information as possible about the family system during this session. It may well be that it is not appropriate to have all the family members present for all the sessions, but it is important that this is acknowledged by the workers and with the family. For example, if sexual issues need to be discussed with the parents later in the work, it may be appropriate for them to have one or two sessions on their own with the workers, and the children join in again after that.

It is obviously also vital that the workers get to the session on time!

RULES OF EFFECTIVE COMMUNICATION

Teaching the family members to improve their communication with each other is fundamental, and intrinsic to all phases of the work. Ways of doing this are widely documented in a number of sources (Egan 1975; Becvar 1974).

The workers will need to discover those behaviours which are the most disabling when the family are communicating. They can then decide which of the following rules of effective communication they need to teach that particular family in more detail. For example, in the Bailey family the shouting was particularly important. In another family it may be their blaming that makes it difficult for them to change.

Equally, some families will need less time spent on communicating effectively than others and the workers will need to decide if they should help the family improve their communication as a focus of the work or not.

It is wise to set the ground rules from the start, then there is a base from which to work. The introduction, engaging the family, and making a contract will all be done (as will the rest of the work) using the basic tools of effective communication. The family will learn more quickly if they can see the workers behaving in this way, and can copy them – this is known as 'modelling'.

The ability to listen is vital in any work with clients, and family work is no exception. It is important to develop the skills of listening to the content of what the family members are saying, and at the same time of observing their behaviour. In this way it is possible to build up a picture of the verbal and non-verbal communication, and whether they convey similar messages. If the verbal and non-verbal messages match, the communication is termed 'congruent'. If this is not the case, it is termed 'incongruent'. When communication is incongruent it is very confusing because the recipient perceives two different messages at once, and it is difficult to know which one to respond to, first.

For example, a family member may be sitting bolt upright, arms folded and with clenched teeth saying ' I am not angry with you'. His non-verbal behaviour tells the participants in the session that he is very angry indeed. In this situation, it is useful for the workers to tackle the subject directly and share their confusion. A worker may say 'Colin, you look very angry to me, which I can understand, yet you say you are not. Which message do you mean to convey?'

The basic ground rules of communication apply equally to workers and to the family: look and speak directly to each other, everybody should speak for themselves, and everybody should be able to make personal or 'I' statements. It is important to describe behaviour rather than ascribe feelings, and to be specific. Positive rephrasing is vital in order to elicit a prescription for change for the better.

Speaking directly

It is useful for the workers to start work with the family as they mean to go on. This entails them taking the initiative on arrival by introducing themselves. They then ensure that they say a few words to each member of the family. This reinforces the message that each family member is important, and the workers expect to communicate with each one directly. If small children are present, the worker should bend down in order to establish eye contact on the same level. They should be offered drawing materials, or other appropriate playthings, through which they can express their feelings. The workers should remember to use language that the children can understand.

Speaking for themselves

It is important to ensure, from the beginning, that when each family member is addressed directly (by the workers or any other family member) they have a chance to speak for themselves. It is quite common for parents to answer for their children for example, or for a 'coping' member of the family to answer for a 'sick' member. For instance, if a worker asks Johnnie, 'Johnnie, what do you enjoy doing in the evenings?'

his mother may answer, 'He likes going to the youth club'. One way of dealing with this is to address Johnnie directly again, but incorporating his mother's response. The worker could say 'Johnnie, your mother says that you enjoy going to the youth club. Is that the only thing you do in the evenings, or are there other things you enjoy doing as well?' In this way it is possible to stick to talking directly to Johnnie, and to ask for a direct response from him, without disqualifying his mother's contribution. This is known as 'checking out', and is useful in many situations.

Making 'I' statements

A development of this is to teach the family members 'to own' their feelings and statements by prefacing comments with the personal pronoun 'I'. Johnnie's response in the previous example could be 'the youth club is nice', but by either gentle probing, or asking family members to copy the workers directly, Johnnie could be encouraged to change his response to 'I like going to the youth club on Thursdays because I like disco dancing'. Teaching family members to communicate in this way is also an important step in the process of changing a blaming response into a specific request for a change. For example, Johnnie's mother could say 'I don't like Johnnie going to the youth club because he mixes with the wrong type of boys there'. If Johnnie's mother was asked by the workers to explain how it made her feel, rather than blaming Johnnie for his behaviour, her response could be 'I don't like Johnnie going to the youth club because I worry that he will get into more trouble on his way home'. This can then be construed as a caring response, because Johnnie's mother is concerned about him and a more positive discussion can ensue.

Often, in a situation where the workers are taking the initiative in this way, the family members learn first to communicate more effectively directly with the workers. It may be more difficult, however, for them to apply the same rules to the other members of their family. It is important for the workers to be aware of this, and ensure that the family members practise this in the session. The family members will then let go of communicating 'through' the workers. Using the same example, Johnnie may say to the workers 'I like going to the youth club on Thursday night, but I like cycling with my mates better'. Johnnie may then need encouragement to say this directly to his mother.

Describing behaviour, not ascribing feelings

Another way of teaching the family to communicate more accurately is if they learn to describe behaviour, rather than ascribe feelings. This helps to take the blaming–labelling element out of their responses, and gives each member space and permission to say what they really think and feel, instead of assumptions being made by the rest of the family. This is particularly important for the index member, and gives that person a chance to do things differently, rather than being stuck in his/her role.

For example, Mr and Mrs Franklin had two daughters, Sarah aged 15 and Karen aged 13. Sarah had been truanting from school and her parents felt she was disobedient and troublesome. Karen, on the other hand, was attending school regularly, getting on well, and was perceived by her parents as 'no trouble'. During a session, Sarah sat still in her chair looking at her feet and did not answer when spoken to directly. Mr Franklin's response was, 'There she goes again, she is just trying to annoy me'. The workers said 'Sarah, you obviously don't want to talk with us at the moment. Is that because you're fed up, or angry, or is it because you want to watch TV instead?' This gave Sarah space to admit that she was fed up, because she felt her father blamed her unfairly. A constructive dialogue between them with the workers' assistance then ensued.

Being specific

Another very important ground rule is 'be specific'. It is very difficult to work with generalizations, as the family members cannot respond positively to each other (even with help!) if they do not know what response is being asked of them. Again, behaviour should be described in ways which people can act on, thus making change achievable.

For example, when asking a mother what, in the family, she would like changed for the better, she may answer 'I would like to be happy'. This gives the other members of the family no clue as to what they can actually do to enable her to 'be happy'. However, if they know exactly what she means they will know how to react. The workers' response to this could be to ask for more detail about what exactly she means, keeping the possibilities to practical issues which are current. It may be useful to give her a few examples. The worker may say to her, 'What exactly do you mean Mrs Bernard – do you mean for example that you'd like to go out with your husband more often, or would you like more help with the household chores?'

By a process of gentle but firm probing, asking the questions 'What' and 'How' it will be possible to elicit a specific request. This can then be the basis for negotiation with the relevant family members. For example, Mrs Bernard's response after this process could be 'I'd like to go to see a film with my husband on Friday night'. This can then lead to negotiation about who could baby-sit, will work be finished in time, which film they would like to see, and so on. It is worth noting that many women who have been used to putting the wishes of their husband and families before their own for many years need a good deal of encouragement to identify what they want for themselves, and furthermore, to ask for it.

Positive rephrasing

An essential part of this progress of changing confused, blaming communication into messages that can be translated into positive action is to teach the family to paraphrase their statements positively. This again should be taught throughout the session, starting at the very beginning. One of the first questions the workers ask the family members is 'What do you enjoy doing?', or 'What are you good at?' When the workers have given the family the idea that they do have strengths, it is possible to continue teaching them to communicate amongst themselves more positively. For example, when the workers are trying to elicit what the family members want to change, it is useful to encourage them to say what they do want, rather than what they don't want. For example, the workers asked Mrs Wright the question 'What would you like to see changed for the better in the family?' and she replied 'I want Angela and Joyce (her daughters) to stop fighting all the time'. The workers' response was 'Do you mean you would like them to get on better together Mrs Wright?' This response both re-phrased the question, and checked out the accuracy of the workers' re-phrasing. This was then encouraged further by the workers until Mrs Wright said 'I wish I could trust Angela to take Joyce to school safely'. This response is one that, again, can be used as a basis for negotiation towards an achievable aim.

ENGAGING THE FAMILY

Direct contact with each of the family members during the session is essential. Having direct contact serves several functions. It enables the workers to observe the patterns of communication between the family members, both verbal and non-verbal. This is the basis for observing the process of family interaction. It also serves to engage each member in work, and it has the effect of taking the pressure off the index member. This is all part of the 'joining' process, which Minuchin identifies as 'the therapist's method of creating a therapeutic system and positioning himself as its leader' (Minuchin 1974).

It may sound simple to establish direct contact with family members, but it can be very difficult to ensure that each family member has enough of the workers' attention. Every social worker is familiar with the feeling of being swamped by demands for attention from one or two family members at the expense of the others, and being immobilized as a result. However, there are ways of selecting not only which issues are discussed, but who discusses them.

One useful technique to control which issues are discussed is to listen to, and acknowledge what the family member is saying, but to delay dealing with that issue until later in the session, or until another session. Of course the issue must be dealt with as the worker promised and not forgotten! For example, in the first session with the Norris family, the workers asked Mrs Norris what she enjoyed doing, in order to elicit her strengths. Mrs Norris's response was 'Never mind about that, I'm fed up with Sonia staying out too late at night. She only does it to cause me trouble'. The worker then said 'I understand that Sonia's behaviour is the most worrying thing for you, and we will be discussing that later. But to do that I need to get to know you all better and I would like to hear what you enjoy doing in your spare time'.

Another useful technique is to ask each family member questions in turn. This serves to make each of them feel that their contribution is valued, and also helps the worker avoid getting stuck listening to one or two family members for a disproportionate amount of time. The families usually soon get to know the rules!

For example, again referring to the Norris family's strengths, Mrs Norris said that she enjoyed going to visit her mother on Sundays. As soon as she had said this, she again brought up the issue about Sonia's lateness. The workers response was 'I did say we will discuss that issue later Mrs Norris, and we will. I have heard the things that you and Ronnie enjoy doing, so now I'd like to hear from Sonia what she enjoys'. Ronnie then interjected, 'Go on Sonia, its your turn now'.

These techniques enable the workers to identify a number of issues that need to be discussed, apart from the presenting problem, and they are therefore able to select small achievable tasks to work on first. In this way the family learns that they are capable of making changes for the better. The major areas of conflict can then be introduced further on in the sessions when the family are feeling safe to change.

Another part of the process of joining, is identifying the authority structure of the family and working with it, before trying to re-examine it. As Minuchin said 'To join a family system, the therapist must accept the family's organization and style, and blend with them' (Minuchin 1974). For example, in the Kent family, Mr Kent usually decided what time the children should be in. During the first session Mr Kent said 'You are the social worker, you tell us what time Mark should be in at night'. The worker's response was 'As Mark's father, what *you* say about that is the most important thing'.

It is also useful during this process to reiterate and link different family members' contributions where possible, as the workers did with the Bailey family. This serves to emphasize the bonds that exist between the family members, or identify bonds that the family members do not usually acknowledge. It also emphasizes the workers' link with the family members, and is a way of clarifying and focusing the workers' minds so it is easier to remember each person's contribution later.

For example, in the Shaw family, Mr Shaw and Paul, his son aged 14, had a difficult relationship and argued frequently. During the first session, Mr Shaw said that he would like to be able to go to the 'pub' with his mates more often, and Paul said he wanted to be able to play his music more often. The workers said 'Mr Shaw and Paul would both like to have more time to themselves – (speaking directly to Mr Shaw) you Mr Shaw would like to go and have a drink with your friends, and (speaking directly to Paul) you Paul would like to go upstairs and listen to your music'. This had the added effect of enabling the family to perceive Mr Shaw and Paul as having something in common.

If there are several children in the family, it is easy for the workers to focus their attention on the adults and index member to the exclusion of the other children who may be there. However young children are, they have a role in the family, and can give the workers valuable information by their behaviour, even if they are too young to speak. For example, during the first session with the Crow family, the workers saw that the parents were having marital difficulties, although the reason for their referral was the 'hyper-activity' of their 2-year-old son, Tim. Their daughter Helen aged 8 was said to be 'good'. The workers noticed that each time Mr and Mrs Crow started disagreeing, Tim created a diversion and demanded their attention in some way. He ran across the room, threw toys, climbed on a chair, and so on. The workers felt that the effect of Tim's behaviour was to ensure that Mr and Mrs Crow did not continue with their disagreement, which could have turned into a full-scale fight.

Equally, children can be very useful allies for the workers. They can almost invariably give a good deal of information about the family process, and often do. Their views of the difficulties and ideas of how to resolve them can be illuminating – often for the family as well as for the workers! If it is inappropriate for younger children to be involved in the discussion at any particular point, it is a good idea to set them a task which relates to it, and this can be shared with the rest of the family later. For example, Mr and Mrs Paul had two daughters aged 13 and 14, and two younger children of 6 and 7. The family had several 'part-time' members, including an older sister who was married but spent a good deal of time in the family home and an aunt. Mr Paul spent a lot of time away and had left the family a number of times in the past for various lengths of time. While this difficult issue was being discussed with Mr and Mrs Paul and the two elder girls, the two younger children were given paper and crayons by one of the workers. They were asked to each draw a picture of the house they would most like to live in, and the family members who would live in it. This kept them occupied while adult discussion was in progress, but the workers were able to introduce their drawings into the discussion in a positive way at the appropriate time.

DRAWING UP A CONTRACT

From the information that the workers have been gathering throughout the session, they can now move on to making a contract or mutual agreement with the family. This will involve everybody in understanding and agreeing about the aims of the work, the duration of the contract, and who will be involved. The workers have already elicited from the family members what they want changed for the better, and have linked these where possible.

The next stage is reiterating with the family the changes they would like to see, or areas of work to be done. It is often useful to write these down as a sort of 'shopping list', and the family can be encouraged to do this during the session. In this way everybody can see that their contribution is included, and it can be checked out whether anybody has any additions or modifications. Obviously other areas of work that emerge during later sessions can be added and dealt with at the time. However, the most important principle at this stage is that the initial areas of work are openly acknowledged and agreed by everybody. When making the list, it is vital to stick to the principle of starting with small achievable steps. This can revive the family's hope that the situation can improve, and even one small achievement reinforces further steps. The workers therefore need to ensure that the list begins with the tasks that need less change and that the major conflict areas come later. Remember, the issues should all be phrased in positive ways. For example, the list at the end of the first session with the Hall family was as follows:

(i) Sunday washing up – who can help Mrs Hall?
(ii) TV – how can Margaret see her favourite programme, at least sometimes?
(iii) How can Mr and Mrs Hall have an evening out together?

(iv) Football – how can Mr Hall take Danny to a match?

(v) Should Danny stay in the family or come into care?

The ranking of the issues is obviously dependent on which is the most important for that particular family. In the example above, there is something for everybody, but the workers were keen to include the scapegoat – Danny – in tasks related to the other members of the family first. This was so the family could view him more positively before the potentially explosive areas of his relationship with his father and possible rejection by the family were tackled.

It is not always possible to get as far as this in the first session, and it may be more appropriate to stick to a few areas of work that are agreed during the discussion. The workers can then go away and either prepare a draft list themselves, or set the family the task of making the list before the next session. It may equally be appropriate to deal with this phase at the beginning of the second session.

Having decided how to handle the agreement about the areas of work, the workers are then in a position to make an offer to work with the family for a number of sessions. Experience shows that it is useful to specify the actual number, rather than a period of time – for example the offer could be for six sessions rather than for three months. When deciding how many sessions to offer a family there is no magic number. Workers will wish to decide how many sessions to offer depending on their own style of work and on the family's needs. However, some may rather not offer a specific number. The length of the contract will then be reviewed during the work or at the follow-up session – usually held two to three months later – although discussion to extend the number of sessions or make further contracts can take place at any time.

Contracting helps both the workers and the family to stick to the agreement. It also means that if a session has to be cancelled for some reason, everybody knows where they are in the process of the work and that, for example, the second session will be next week instead of this week. Usually by the time the family get to a statutory social work agency they are in considerable difficulty. It is very often easier in these circumstances for them to accept a finite contract rather than a more traditional open-ended offer of help. For example, if they are offered six sessions aimed at improving their situation, they may feel that the position they are in at the moment could not be worse, so it would be 'worth a try'. Families often agree to work on this basis.

It is important that each individual involved is asked directly for their agreement to work. If some family members are unsure, they can be given time to consider it, and the workers can contact them to find out their decision. The workers need to decide whose involvement is crucial. They gave thought to this during the planning stage but it will take some negotiation with the family if not everybody is prepared to join in. If everybody agrees, then the practicalities of the timing of the sessions can be arranged.

It is worth saying that if the workers are positive about what they can offer, reluctant members are often persuaded by them. It is also useful to make a regular time and day if possible, which is easy for everyone to remember, and again helps to add some structure to the work.

□□ (e) Activities for further learning

1 Discuss with a colleague or in a group the following interventions using the references offered for each:

   (a) Modelling and instruction (Bandura 1971; Corsini 1966: 84–103)
   (b) Decentralizing the index member (Haley and Hoffman 1967: 97–103)
   (c) The process of contracting (Andolfi 1979: 33–48; Hutton 1977; Seabury 1976).

2 In pairs, one person looks at and speaks directly to the other, asking what he/she is good at. This should last for about five minutes, then the other one repeats the exercise.

3 Again in pairs:
   (a) Choose an issue that one person wants to discuss. The other's task is to elicit what the first person enjoys doing.
   (b) Spend five minutes with one person trying to discuss his/her 'burning issue' and the other acknowledging this but delaying any response. Then change roles and repeat the process.
   (c) Tell each other how you felt during the exercise.

4 In a group:
   (a) One member of the group gives a problem statement relating to another member of the group, such as 'Diane, you talk too much'. The next person then has the task of rephrasing this positively, for example, 'You, Kay, would prefer it if Diane listened more'. Everyone in the group can then take turns in making a problem statement and the next converting it to a prescription of action.
   (b) Continue (a) but in addition to the prescription, the next person has to design a task out of the prescription. To extend the example, when Diane is spoken to directly she will silently count to five before replying. This gives her time to concentrate on what she has heard before responding.

8 / WARMING UP

This chapter is dedicated to the warming-up phase which took place during the workers' second interview with the Bailey family. We discuss the analysis of previous information, the use of metaphors and analogies, and how to offer appropriate tasks as the workers warm up the family for the crucial change that follows. But first let us join the workers' thoughts as they prepared to meet the Bailey family for the second time.

*   *   *

PUTTING THE INFORMATION TOGETHER AND FORMING THE WARM-UP FOCUS

It seemed that we had begun to show the family members different ways of communicating and there were initial signs that they wanted to learn them. After all, they did not have to let us take so much of the lead. Similarly, it seemed that we had already begun to make some contact with family members. By sharing our attention with each of them equally we had started to make Mary less central in the family. The family also accepted our 'contract'. We reflected upon what we now knew about them. By the end of the first interview we hope to have gathered some information about at least five issues:

1 The family's definitions of their aspirations and difficulties.
2 The family's description of the ways in which they have tried to handle the conflict for which they are currently seeking help. This data is often sought, particularly by behaviourists (e.g. Patterson 1971).
3 What communication patterns we could observe in this family. Here we follow Satir's (1967) approach most of all.
4 What alliances we could observe in this family. This is related to the concept of 'structural orientation', as developed by Minuchin (1974).

5 Any inference we could hazard about a hidden (unacknowledged and/or unresolved) conflict that would explain seemingly irrational behaviour in the family. Here, more psychodynamic concepts are used (e.g. Pincus and Dare 1978 relates to this case).

On the basis of information we had gathered during our first interview with the Baileys we knew that:

1 All family members wanted to have more 'good times' outside the home, but the parents thought that the children's pursuits were too risky and the children's behaviour seemed to the parents such that the parents did not feel free to have any time away from them.

2 When the children did come home in time neither of the parents would pay attention to them. It was only when they were late that attention was offered, in the form of reprimand and punishment from both parents.

3 Most of the content of family communication centred on reprimand, anger, accusations of misconduct, and mockery.

4 Although the children were continuously fighting amongst themselves, they joined together in a powerful alliance against their parents, with the edge of it being directed towards Mr Bailey, at whom they would openly swear.

5 Both parents gave the children quite a lot materially in clothes, toys, and pocket money. Indeed this was all that the children ever asked for. Yet none of the children seemed to express warmth, let alone gratitude for these things. We wondered, therefore, if we should infer that material things were being used to compensate for something else lacking in this family. If so, what was being compensated for? Was the crisis of four years ago left unspoken and/or unresolved, and were the parents still attempting to counter its effects by giving the children clothes, toys, and pocket money? (see e.g. Bentovim, 1979).

FOCUSING AND PLANNING OUR INTERVENTIONS: THE IMPORTANCE OF HAVING FUN

Choosing the first focus is a jig-saw puzzle exercise. On returning for the second interview we still want to engage the whole family. First, we need to take them through a relatively light and safe exercise that ensures that they learn to communicate with each other constructively in our absence between sessions. It is important to warm up the family to the possibility of change: many family work programmes have been stopped by the family members because the work immediately raised such painful issues that the members could not handle them between sessions – in other words, the workers immediately approached a crucial focus. Because of this danger, we feel obliged to choose the first focus with the utmost care.

*

We asked ourselves what would be an improved communication pattern among the Baileys. We remembered clearly the frequent bursts of accusations and reprimands, with Mary swearing at her father or depreciative comments flying in all directions.

Regardless of possible causes for such agonizing family life, it seemed necessary for us to cool the atmosphere somewhat and explore alternatives that might open the way for the discussion of the present or past conflicts, or both. The expression of affection, appreciation, and fun could be a marked yet safe contrast to explore, but how could we engage the Baileys in an attempt to communicate appreciation, affection, and smiles? The answer to this had to be found in the words that the Baileys had used, not in our words. We had somehow to 'reframe' what they had said, so that it contained the seeds for new behaviours, those that would enable them to achieve what they wanted. Of course, it is useless to come back and say 'you need to express more appreciation, affection, and fun to each other'. In fact, it rarely helps to say to people that they should express any feelings. It is better to suggest to them something to *do*. The particular activity is selected and introduced in such a way that it will lead the members to express the avoided feelings.

Now, what had each of the Baileys said they enjoyed and what would they like to have more of? We remembered from the first interview that:

— Tony liked to go to the park with his mates and play football;
— Mrs Bailey enjoyed reading and listening to music;
— Di wanted to go out, anywhere, and she enjoyed learning history;
— Mr Bailey enjoyed sports, particularly darts and swimming;
— Mary wanted to go to the disco;
— Don favoured woodwork and football;
— Jim loved riding his tricycle.

When we reflected on what these might have in common, there were a number of answers. For example, most of these were recreational activities of short duration which family members pursued on their own, mostly outside the home.

*

We also recalled that when we had proceeded to ask them what each hoped for, six types of replies had been given:

— Di did not know. We did not press her, but requested her to think about it further for the next session.
— Mary wanted to return to her previous school. It was too early for us to comment on this issue so we said that we would talk about it later.
— Both Mr and Mrs Bailey wanted the children to do what they were told.
— Mrs Bailey added that she would like to go out with her husband.
— Mr Bailey said that he wanted to spend more time with the children.
— Tony and Don wanted to have more time to play football freely.

It was clear that we would not be able to respond to six requests at once. Instead we wanted to focus the family on one. Light activity seemed to be something they all enjoyed. They had not found a way of enjoying it together, as one group, yet Mr Bailey was clearly interested. It seemed that we might get his support if we tried to introduce a joint fun activity. If this could be done it would provide us with plenty of opportunities to give examples and to encourage the communication of appreciation, affection, and fun among family members. It would also enable us to observe what happens between family members when they attempt to have fun together. So we decided to approach first the communication of appreciation, affection, and smiles. We decided to do this by offering the family a game. The game was for each of them to write on a piece of paper what they wished for the other and what they would like to do for the other. Then the notes would be folded and put together (good games need the element of suspense). After that we would draw out each note and read it aloud. Each member would then have the opportunity to respond to the 'present' sent to him or her.

Let us consider this 'present-giving game' in some detail.

(i)   The game involved all the family members.

(ii) It was something they could all do – it was an achievable task.

(iii) It could be said to be what many of them wanted anyhow. We came back and said, 'you all said that you wanted to have more fun. Let us have some fun here together'. The first sentence ('you wanted to have more fun') was simply a summary of what the Baileys had said. The second included the art of 'reframing'. We put the 'fun' into a different frame; instead of outside the home and separately, inside and together.

(iv) The game created a situation which was likely to give us opportunities to intervene and gently focus interaction around a selected behaviour – the communication of appreciation, affection, and smiles – to show these feelings ourselves, to encourage their expression by family members, and to observe exactly what is done by whom to prevent it.

(v)   Lastly, the present-giving game delayed certain issues from being taken up immediately, such as the more painful and individualized ones. The present conflict was not raised; neither was it likely that the past conflict would emerge. The children's abuse of Mr Bailey was kept in abeyance, as were Mary's special difficulties. All these could be part of a crucial focus to be taken up later. At this stage we were still preparing the ground and insisting on approaching difficulties in a certain order. The big 'drama' was to be handled only after this session.

22 March

Second family interview: WARMING UP – *the use of fun in aid of communication*

We have already described the process of planning our second interview with the Baileys. The present-giving game we offered the family is one of many activities that are used by group and family therapists to accelerate communication. It seems to help growth, hence the name 'growth game'. Essentially, the idea is to suggest to people to join in an activity that can be light and amusing. The activity leads to experimentation with new ways of expression. The Baileys became rather involved in writing the notes containing the wishes they had for each other, although they found this game quite difficult to carry through. When it came to reading the messages aloud, we tried to help them by encouraging each to also express the feeling he/she had about receiving the 'present'. In this way we began to train them to express their own feelings. There were some initial attempts to do this, but the growing warmth was quickly swept aside by intense exchanges of abuse and accusations among the children. We still did not attempt to deal with the anger directly in spite of the fact that when we left the home we both felt extremely shattered and agonized by what we had heard. In this interview we remained with the goal of warming up. We gave the family a 'job to do till we meet next week'. This homework task was to write up on a large sheet of paper, which we helped them to hang up, what was good about each of them. They seemed to be interested in this task and we hoped that it would show us where praise and warmth had been directed within the family.

*   *   *

□□ (a) Summary: what the workers did

Planning

1 The workers carefully collated all the information gathered previously. This concerned five aspects: (a) the family's definitions of their aspirations and difficulties; (b) behavioural aspects; (c) communication patterns; (d) structural issues; and (e) psychodynamic implications.

2 The workers matched what the family wanted with their own ideas of how this might come about by designing a task that satisfied five conditions: (a) it involved the whole family; (b) it was achievable – something they could all do; (c) it was an activity that all of them wanted in different ways; (d) it was an activity that allowed the workers to introduce the new communication behaviour they thought would help; and (e) it concentrated the family on warming up and delayed handling difficult issues prematurely.

During the session

3 The workers linked their plan to the first session by reminding the family there was a common thread in their wishes – one way or another they all wanted to have fun.

4 The workers then suggested a change of context to the family wishes by offering to have fun together (rather than apart) and at home (instead of outside).

5 As the present game task was going on, the workers encouraged and praised new communication behaviour – the expression of appreciation and smiles among members of the family.

6 At the same time the workers observed the difficulties family members presented in exchanging appreciation.

7 However, the workers held back from responding to the above difficulties during this session.

8 Instead, they continued to focus the family on warming up and left with them a homework task that extended the new communication behaviour into the period between sessions.

☐☐ (b) How else could the situation have been handled?

Another game that would have served a similar function would be the 'cushion game': all the family members and workers stand in a circle. A cushion is thrown (gently!) among participants and the thrower of the cushion makes an appreciative statement directly to the recipient, about them. For example, 'Billy, thank you for helping me with the washing up' or 'Jane, I am glad you were in on time from school today', and so on. The recipient then throws the cushion to any other participant at random, and repeats the process. This means that like the other game, the family members learn to:

- communicate positively with each other,
- listen to each other,
- have fun together.

Again, this game takes place in the session so that the workers are available for help throughout.

The 'speaker's chair' game is also a task that can be set for all the family by the workers, with the same aims in mind. In this game, one chair in the room is designated as 'the speaker's chair' and only the person sitting in the chair can speak. The task for each family member in turn is to sit in the chair, and say something positive about one of the others. For example, 'I like it when Dad takes me to the park to play football'. One way that this game can be modified is to ask a parent to direct the game. It may be useful for the workers to start off, and then hand over to the parents once they are clear what is necessary. For example, one parent could be asked to choose who sits in the chair, and the other one to choose whom they speak about. This development serves various additional functions: it reinforces parental authority; it encourages the parents to both co-operate together and control the children; and it could have been linked with Mr and Mrs Bailey's stated wish, that the children do as they tell them. This task teaches the family to communicate positively about each other, and additionally ensures that each person is carefully listened to by the others.

A different out-of-session task that could have been used would be to arrange a simple outing together; for example, to the local park. This again would link the family's expressed wish to have fun and enable them to practise some of the things learnt in the session.

☐☐ (c₁) The use of metaphors and the warm-up focus: some basic issues

The workers with the Baileys listened carefully to the family's aspirations as well as to their definition of their difficulties. The workers then asked themselves: 'What communication pattern do the family members actually use in pursuing their goals?' Having a problem usually means that a certain behaviour is either absent or misused in linking the 'problem' with the desired outcome: the thread connecting behaviour is tangled. The 'connecting strategy' adopted by the family (in the Bailey case, anger and sending out), is disabling (Gordon 1978: 40–8). The worker can use a task or game to find out exactly what it is the family members do when the opportunity to achieve their goals is available. The task or game, however brief, is a metaphor which gives the worker an effective means of observing this process *in vivo*. It creates space for experimentation with a new 'connecting strategy'. As this is attempted by the family the disabling strategy is likely to surface, yet it will do so safely within the 'unreal' realm of metaphor.

*

We have all benefited from myths, fairy tales, and metaphors as a means of learning, developing imagination, and changing ideas. Aesop's *Fables*, *Mother Goose*, the story of Achilles, each in its own way helps to mould our ideas, teach us by example and thereby affect our behaviour and view of the world. By using analogies we can reason from parallel cases; metaphors give us a means of speaking of one thing in terms of another providing a new dimension to what is being described; symbols help us to represent what we wish to say in different ways, both verbally and through actions. They all enrich our communication and have the potential of creating new ways of looking at something familiar, or of making new links not previously seen. They therefore have the potential of helping to promote change by encouraging the individual to broaden his/her perceptions and views.

By listening carefully to what a family is saying, the worker collects several leads which may be possible to link together into common themes. For example, the common theme in the Bailey family was 'having fun'. It should be remembered that 'the most important requirement for an effective metaphor is that it meets the client at his model of the world ... The significant factors in the metaphor are the client's interpersonal relationships and patterns of coping within the context of the problem'. (Gordon 1978: 19).

The development of analogies and metaphors follows from the worker's ability to hold on to and make sense of the information collected from the various levels of communication existing within sessions. Families try to tell us what is troubling them in all sorts of ways – by what they say and what they do (Haley 1976: Chapter 3). The worker is asking herself all the time, what else are they trying to tell me, show me, make me feel, so that I can help them change? Linking previously unconnected communications, or expressing the issues in different images often enable the family to get out of entrenched modes of thinking about a problem, which in turn helps to promote change. From the first contact with the family, the worker is collecting information, gaining a sense of the family's language and style of communication. The worker allows her senses to absorb this information so that she can then sift through and find the links. Before the worker can formulate a metaphor she must listen to all the family is trying to convey. Linking attempts are going on in the worker's mind concomitantly as she finds the moment to reframe adequately an aspect of the problem.

Analogies are used for different purposes and they vary tremendously as to their detail and depth. The present-giving game which the workers used with the Baileys avoided the detail of family relationships and remained on the surface of 'anger' versus 'fun'; avoiding, for the time being, the exclusion of father and the 'game of sending out'. This was a reflection of the workers' understanding of the therapeutic aim during the phase of warming up. The workers were aware very early in their contact that this family were having difficulty communicating. The workers might have utilized their observation that the family's language of accusations and quarrels were 'well oiled' by stating this to them. In this way they would have been letting the family know that they sensed the nature of the difficulties while giving them all some common language within which it would be possible to speak about this sensitive area. The family could then have been able to check out what exactly was required – oiling up? unfreezing? a complete overhaul? As this is a delicate area for the family, to discuss it straight away, and directly, could increase anxiety and prevent progress. By speaking of it in terms of this analogy, or another, the workers may enable the family to think about painful issues in more comfortable language. Children especially enjoy this form of communication and often add their own images, amending and elaborating the original. In this way it is possible to capture the family's imagination and interest in an otherwise 'no go' territory.

This example differs from the one used with the Baileys in another way. While the workers suggested to the Baileys a game, a form of action, the later example is one of a verbal-symbolic form of communication. Indeed, analogies can vary not only in detail and depth, but also with regard to the mode of expression used to convey them. It is important that the worker chooses that mode of expression which appeals to the family to ensure their receptivity to the message. In Chapter 9 we shall discuss the use of structural analogies as a particularly important means of communication for local authority social workers.

□□ (d₁) A different example related to the use of symbolic analogies

A young mother contacted the Social Services Department expressing concern for her marriage. After several sessions it was arranged for the worker to meet the couple together. The worker was aware of the couple's ambivalence and anxiety about talking together due to their fear of what might happen. However, they responded positively to the worker's offer of further sessions, the worker's hunch about their ambivalence was not made explicit. An appointment was scheduled for the following week. The next day however, the wife came into the office in a panic – their ceiling had fallen in, the flat was structurally dangerous, they needed a builder immediately. The worker privately wondered why the wife had come to her instead of going direct to the landlord? She offered to go to the flat with the wife and to help the couple contact the landlord. Within supervision the worker continued to explore how this experience fitted into her work with this couple and in what way the communication could be used symbolically. During her next session she used the experience of the previous week, linking it with the notion of ambivalence which she had sensed existed between them. She did this by talking simply in terms of the couple's 'marital house which needed restructuring', their urgent need for a 'proper builder' who would make their 'marital home' safe and sound. She extended this analogy further by wondering with them about their questions of what sort of builder she was; did she know how to fix structures without making the whole thing fall apart?

Linking external realities with the internal worries in this way is often helpful to families who cannot find the words to express the extent of their worries and need the worker to do this for them. It was through the panic and worry of the ceiling incident that the couple were able to communicate to their worker the depth of their fear over the restructuring work needed within their marriage. Open to all levels of communications from her clients, the worker was able to hear the message sufficiently to wonder about it further within supervision, thus enabling her to hear the symbolic message in a live and vivid way. Afterwards she was able to link and use the symbols within the situation. The worker chose to use this as a means of talking to the couple about a delicate matter before the work of change could begin. She could have also chosen to introduce a further image with an 'as if' phrase: 'It's as if you are afraid of being a Humpty Dumpty family which all the King's Men could not put together again.' This image introduces the aspect of power and authority which may have been helpful if the worker believed that this was part of the couple's reluctance to work with her.

The degree to which workers will choose symbols or activities to convey analogies will vary with their individual style in combination with the culture of the family and the nature of the problems to be tackled. Of course, activities and verbal interventions are not mutually exclusive; indeed, they complement one another. Workers need to learn about their own style and how it can be extended to meet the needs of the families with which they work. The worker's repertoire will develop over time for these skills can be acquired and mastered with practice. We return to the use of analogies in Chapter 9. Before we do this, it is important to remember that having designed an analogic task, the worker needs to deliver it successfully. We shall therefore talk about tasks and contracts more specifically.

☐☐ (c₂) Tasks and contracts of the warm-up phase: some basic issues

Tasks can be used to further various aims in work with families (Andolfi 1979: Chapter 4), and we will look at other ways of using them below; warm-up tasks are usually aimed at an improvement of communication in the family. A directive is given to make people behave differently, to intensify the relationship between the family and the worker, and to gather information (Haley 1976: 52–8). It is also used to dramatize family transactions, and to suggest change in this way (Minuchin 1974: 150).

Some basic principles to bear in mind when designing tasks are:

PURPOSEFULNESS

Like all techniques, tasks and games should only be used to further the worker's aims within the overall plan of work with the family. There is no point in setting tasks for the sake of it, anymore than there is in sculpting, making an interpretation, moving chairs, or using any other technique. It is crucial to have clear and specific aims.

WORK WITH WHAT THE FAMILY GIVE YOU

We have talked about teaching the family to listen to each other in Chapter 7, but one of the first things the worker must do is to listen *to them*. The worker needs to find out what their views are, what developmental stage they have reached, and about their perception of the situation. In this way the worker can respect and utilize what the family thinks is important (Haley 1976). It is only once this information has been elicited that the worker can clarify it and use it to work out tasks that will mean something to the family, that they can identify with and as a result be motivated to do. It is only if these things happen that the family members will be able to feel safe enough to begin to change their pattern of communication and then feel there is something in it for them.

WORK WITH THE WHOLE FAMILY

It is important to design tasks that every member of the family is motivated to do, because the worker aims to effect change in the *whole* family system. This means that each family member should be given a role in the task – even if it is to stay out of it! (Haley 1976). It is useful on occasions to give family members roles as 'helpers' or 'observers' to ensure that everyone is involved. For example, if the tasks set were for the parents to arrange an evening out together, on say, Friday, their son's task could be to ask them on Thursday where they had decided to go; their daughter's task could be to establish whether they had enjoyed themselves, and to report back at the next family session. Remember, 'a good task has something for everyone' (Haley 1976: 58).

SMALL ACHIEVABLE STEPS

When selecting a task, it is important to try and get the right balance between the task being real and achievable for the family, while also stretching them and encouraging them to take risks. It is always wise to ask if the task is really achievable for the family; if not, they may be set up to fail. In other words, if the family do not achieve the task, look at where the worker went wrong, rather than where the family did. When everybody in the family is involved in the task, everybody feels good when it is achieved. At the warm-up phase it is important that the tasks lead to reinforcement of family strengths.

WORKER'S ROLE

It is equally important that the worker feels fairly confident that the task fits her style, that she feels comfortable with it, and that it is right for the family at this point. It is easier for workers to design tasks doing things that they are good at and enjoy. A way of overcoming any apprehension is to use the support systems in the agency – co-worker, support group, or supervisor – to think the task through, and modify it if necessary until it feels right. Some workers find it useful to practise by means of role-play to gain more confidence. In this way the worker can be helped to clarify whether it is her apprehension and the task which needs refining or whether it is actually inappropriate for the family at this point.

BE REALISTIC

There are some good reasons for the family rejecting a task, so in order to ensure that the task is really achievable, the worker must take into consideration as much of the family's world as possible. Areas it is useful to consider are:

The family's resources

These can include their level of self-esteem, the extended family network and expectations, and any other factor that has diminished the family's energy and/or skill.

External factors

These will include the family's housing situation, financial position, the hours the parents work, play facilities, schooling, and so on. It is important to be clear exactly how much control the family or the worker and the agency have over any of these areas. In this way it is possible to be sure that the task is set in a way that is honest, realistic, and viable. When setting an out of session task, it is vital for the workers to go through with the family, in detail, exactly what the task will entail. They will need to decide who will take part, where they will go, when they will go, which way they will go there, and so on. If there is some reluctance, it may also be useful to discuss with them how they will deal with any difficulties that might arise, without being put off the task. Referring to the previous example about an outing to the local park, the family can decide what they will do if it rains, what time the park is open, or what time it gets dark, who will arrange another time if for some reason they cannot go when arranged, and so on. During this process, the worker is able to make sure that the task is one that the family want to do, and also that it is achievable. This is both in terms of the family's motivation, and the external reality. For example, do the father's working hours fit in with the time that the children are off school?

Racial and cultural factors

Local authority social services departments work with families from a wide variety of cultural and ethnic backgrounds, so it is vital to be sensitive to the different expectations and perceptions of situations each individual family may have. For example, workers may need to be aware of different perceptions of parental authority structures, different male and female roles, expectation of control and discipline of children, or possible language difficulty. It is neither possible nor appropriate to generalize about any of these here, but it is crucial to find out about them either from the family or from literature (McGoldrick, Pearce, and Giordiano 1982).

Perceptions of the agency

The family may have had previous experience or knowledge of the agency which may colour their response to the present worker. This may matter particularly in an agency with statutory functions. Again, it is important to be aware of these factors, and if necessary to acknowledge and discuss them with the family before going ahead with the task.

Anticipating the worst

When planning any session it is wise to anticipate a number of possibilities, and decide how to deal with different situations the family may present. This is a useful way of handling the worker's worst fears about the session. For example, what should the response be if the worker arrives in the middle of a family argument; what if the family flatly refuse to do the task that is set for them, and so on.

It is useful to work out under what circumstances the task should be modified, or the session postponed, before the worker approaches the family. For example, should the task go ahead if one parent is not present? By using the support within the agency, that is supervisor, co-worker or support group, the worker can reduce her anxiety about working in a new way, and also identify the reasons if the work plan has to be changed.

MOBILIZING THE FAMILY'S AGREEMENT TO DO THE TASK

There are some ways of helping workers gain confidence in developing more directive approaches with families. One of them is to convince the worker to act as if the family does want to participate in the task or the game. For example, rather than 'Would you like to play a game? We thought we might do this if you agree . . . ', the worker will say, 'Now we are going to play a game, which we will all be involved in'. If the family are apprehensive, it is often useful to fall back on the 'modelling' principle, that is for the workers to do it first themselves. In the tasks outlined above, one of the workers would throw the cushion first, directly addressing one member of the family; in the second one, a worker would sit in the 'speaker's chair' first and make a statement, to get the game going. Confidence and ease are as contagious as the workers' anxiety, so it is better to be positive.

Another way of allaying any anxiety is to define the task as 'silly' or 'crazy'. For example, the worker could say 'You will probably think that this game is crazy, but let's do it anyway'. Therefore, if the family's response is to say that the game is stupid or crazy, then they are already agreeing with what the worker has said, and their fear is overcome (Haley 1976: 57).

Experience shows that if the worker has prepared the task and feels confident enough to try it with the family, it is very unlikely they will refuse to co-operate.

□□ (d₂) A different example related to the use of tasks

Lisa, aged 14, was referred to the Social Services Department by the EWO because the school were worried about her behaviour – not in class, but outside the school premises. She often loitered outside the school gates with a group of girls, and had got into several fights. She had also been seen being met at school and going off with a man aged about 35. The school knew very little about Lisa's home circumstances other than that this man was not a member of the family. They also knew that Lisa had been 'bragging' in school, saying that this man was her boyfriend, but that her grandparents, with whom she lived, did not approve of him.

Lisa's sister, Mary, who lived and worked away from home, also contacted the Department saying that Lisa lived with her grandparents, who were now elderly and could not control Lisa. She said that there were constant arguments at home, and mentioned that Lisa was spending time with a man a good deal older than herself, and that her grandparents were very worried about this. Mary was very concerned about their grandparents, and felt the situation was making them ill. She said that Mr and Mrs Gardner (their grandparents) could not cope with Lisa much longer, and that there was a risk of her having to come into care unless some help could be offered. Mary also said that both Mr and Mrs Gardner and she were very worried that Lisa was at risk of becoming pregnant, or of getting into trouble with the police, or both.

Two workers tackled this situation, having decided to work jointly. They invited Mr and Mrs Gardner, Lisa, and Mary to a family session. They spent the session gathering information, and at the end were able to make an assessment. They were agreed that there were a lot of strengths in the family, that Lisa still wanted to be with her grandparents, and that they still wanted her to live with them. However, it seemed that communication between the family members had broken down, and as a result Lisa was very confused about what was expected of her by her grandparents.

In the second session the workers set a task for the family, which was to draw a geneogram or a family tree. They took with them plenty of paper and felt tip pens, and started the work themselves. One worker explained the task while the other one started drawing the family tree. As they did this, they encouraged all the family members to join in, and soon Lisa was able to do the main part of the drawing. Mr and Mrs Gardner were encouraged to share their knowledge of the family over many years, and were able to explain who was part of the family, how they related to each other, and what happened to them. Mary was also able to add more recent information.

It became clear during the session that Lisa was indeed very confused about her place in the family, and that there were numerous family secrets. Some of these were related to very traumatic incidents which had affected family members, but that had never been openly discussed or acknowledged. Mary too, had been unaware of these incidents, and was equally relieved to discuss them. The family were increasingly able to communicate with each other during the session, and Lisa became relaxed and animated.

By the time the workers went to the third session, it was clear that Lisa's behaviour had improved greatly. Mr and Mrs Gardner and she were able to communicate much more openly, and her grandparents were able to exercise their authority over her more clearly. Although areas of difficulty still existed, Lisa and her grandparents, with her sister's help, had already started negotiating agreements about dealing with these.

In this particular situation, quite a dramatic improvement occurred as a result of one particular task; the drawing of a family tree or geneogram, which can be useful in many situations.

*

□□ **(e) Activities for further learning**

1 **Read about the following interventions and discuss them with your colleagues:**

   (a) **Growth games (Satir 1972; Blatner 1973)**
   (b) **Communication training (Egan 1975)**
   (c) **Homework tasks (Haley 1976: 81–99).**

2 **Re-acquaint yourself with stories by Hans Christian Anderson and the Grimm Brothers. Let yourself relish the imagery and symbolism.**

3 *The animal game.* **Ask yourself, 'What do I feel right now?' Having identified the feeling, think of an animal that would best demonstrate this feeling.**

4 *Practising 'It's as if . . . '.* **Either by yourself or in a group, think of a piece of behaviour. Now think of as many different images which illustrate that same behaviour. If you have done this within a group, compare notes.**

5 **Do some reading to get some ideas about the sorts of tasks and games that workers use, for example, Andolfi (1979: Chapter 4), Peine and Howarth (1975). Then:**

   (a) **Think of a family with whom you are working, and identify those communication behaviours from which they would benefit by learning to do differently; such as listening, 'checking out', being specific, making 'I' statements, etc. (refer to Chapter 7 for different ways of communication).**

   (b) **Using the same family, think of their stated wishes. If this is difficult, choose a topic which will affect every member of the family more or less equally, and which is on fairly neutral territory. An example would be how the family choose the TV programmes they watch. Remember: it is important to avoid major issues of conflict at this stage.**

   (c) **With the help of your group or co-worker, think of a task that will match both (a) and (b) above. Often the simpler the better!**

Continued on next page

Continued from previous page

When doing this exercise, it is useful to clarify:

    (i) **The aim of the task – do you as a worker feel comfortable with it?**

    (ii) **Are you clear about the link between the family's stated aim and your aim?**

    (iii) **Think through how you will present the task to the family, and if you are co-working, which of you will do it.**

    (iv) **Again if you are co-working, decide which worker will take responsibility for each part of the session.**

    (v) **Do not forget the practicalities. Decide what you need, for example, paper, coloured pens, and so on, and who will take them to the session.**

(d) Do it!
It is always useful to practise on your support group using role-play to start with, but you may feel confident enough to go ahead and work directly with a family.

9 / APPROACHING THE CRUCIAL FOCUS

After the second interview family members will communicate with each other more effectively. The ground is ready for mutual support as clarity of expression, needed to approach more painful yet central issues, has grown. The worker too is clearer about the pattern of behaviour that will need to change if the family is to move on. These patterns are usually clustered around a theme which we call 'the crucial focus', since it is a focus central to the family's rules and to its structure (while the initial 'warm-up focus' concerns only its communication culture). However, the worker cannot jump straight into the crucial focus, it has to be approached gradually. We now consider how this may be done. We also make room to consider working with the impasse, using statutory powers, further use of analogies, and dealing with unexpected events.

MAKING A HYPOTHESIS ABOUT THE CRUCIAL FOCUS

After observing the family reactions to the warm-up focus the worker is in a good position to pick up the threads that the family has already offered and tie them together into a hypothesis. The 'focal hypothesis' is the worker's educated guess as to the major blocks in the family system and the forces that sustain it. Arriving at the 'focal hypothesis' is by now common practice in short-term psychotherapy (Small 1979: Chapter 6) and particularly so in family therapy (Bentovim 1979; Weakland *et al*. 1974, Palazzoli *et al*. 1980). Practitioners are guided by different models while they make such hypotheses, and some workers are more systematic than others in formulating them. Psychodynamically oriented workers will tend to assume that the intervention offered as a result is more or less a straightforward reflection of the workers' hypothesis which is usually conveyed to the family in small steps that lead towards the whole formulation shared at the end. More recent approaches make a sharper distinction between the hypothesis and the intervention. These approaches assume that the hypothesis is quite separate from the intervention. Such division seems particularly relevant if the worker wishes to employ a range of activities that stem from the hypothesis and to rely less on the family's awareness. The approach presented in this handbook follows this more diverse style of intervention.

*

We may begin with quite a general and even fairly vague formulation. In fact, the work with the Bailey family is a good example of this. The workers hypothesized only that an event had happened four years previously which was activating certain processes in the present within the Bailey family system. They speculated that the effects of past events were kept alive in the system by the perpetual resorting to anger, by the 'game of sending out' and by the exclusion and abuse of the father. Again, the process by which workers arrive at their focal hypothesis varies considerably. You will have seen that the work with the Baileys, for example, started by spreading the net as widely as possible. The workers began by looking for any information that might lead them to an intervention. Five such areas were on the workers' minds during the first interview: the family's definitions of their aspirations and difficulties; the behavioural patterns in the family; its communication culture; structural alliances; and any irrational behaviour that may signify the operation of unconscious forces in the family system.

The warm-up focus took up only part of this welter of information; it connected the family's aspirations with the workers' judgement of what might improve their communication culture. In order to make a focal hypothesis it is helpful to ask some simple questions. The central one is very non-sensical. Instead of asking, as is commonly done, how the difficulties, including the presenting problem, hurt and disturb family members, it is possible to ask ourselves how they actually help. Our assumption in doing so is that difficulties and problems do not only hurt, but equally help to maintain the family's steady state.

Let us turn to the Bailey family again. The question we ask ourselves is how the shouting, the 'sending out', and the exclusion and abuse of father *help* this family. One way of answering this is to imagine the family members pursuing their aspirations (in the Bailey case, having fun together) while being stripped of their difficulties and problems. In this case, the workers' associations led them to speculate that if this occurred, the memories of what had happened four years previously would come to the surface. These would then be experienced as too painful for family members to handle, let alone share, and members might fantasize about the family falling apart. The persistence of difficulties and problems is thus interpreted as a protection of the family system against a dreaded calamity (Ezriel 1950). The question is, of course, whether the dreaded calamity is a real one – will the family fall apart if the memories are shared. The workers evidently thought that it was not. If they thought that the family could not take the sharing of past events, they would have had to intervene differently. They might have had to find ways of helping the family live with the knowledge that some events in the past would never be shared and that this was all right too. Their 'diagnosis' would have been the same, but their intervention quite different, presumably much more focused on here-and-now strategies that the family members can adopt in order to cope better with unresolved and undisclosed memories. With this in mind, let us see what happened in the third interview.

* * *

29 March

Third family interview: APPROACHING THE CRUCIAL FOCUS – *the more you get the more you demand. What lies behind this?*

We were all waiting in the living room for some ten minutes before Mr Bailey returned from work. We insisted on waiting. When he entered the home Mr Bailey looked surprised that we had waited. Not to wait for him would have amounted to colluding with the family in excluding their father. We were intending, in fact, to involve him even more later on.

We asked to see the chart which we had left with them. A second page had been added to the one we had left, filled with 'thank you for doing . . . ' notes to each other. It was not exactly what we had asked them to do, but there was abundant warmth in it. They seemed to have enjoyed the change, but not for long. Soon flashes of anger started to fly around the room again. This time we could also experience Mr Bailey's flair for calling his son names. The time felt right for a more direct approach, but we proceeded gently at first. We simply expressed our feeling of puzzlement at the frequent intense exchanges of anger. We asked if this had always been so in the family. By doing this we were indeed opening the way for the exploration of the possible influence of the past conflict on the present one. The parents said that earlier years had been happier, and readily narrated the chronology of events. We encouraged them also to describe their own families and the roles they had occupied in them, as is done while building up a geneogram, and to compare them with the present family that they had created. We noticed that they elaborated on how the two of them had met and on the birth of each child. However hardly anything was said about the years between Don's birth and that of Jim. We did not comment on the fact that we knew that the couple had separated for a short time during that period. We listened and just said that it was still puzzling. The parents obviously wanted each of these children to be born and gave them all the material things they asked for, yet the children appeared to express only anger all the time. Why was this? Nobody in the family could answer. We raised the possibility that the children were, in fact, asking for something other than material things but did not know how to say it. Tony and Mary responded with 'perhaps' to this. Di did not know. We suggested that we should meet with Mr and Mrs Bailey alone the following week 'in order to find out how you can help your children to ask for what they really want'. The parents readily consented, as did the children. In fact we were also demonstrating that the parents were the adults in the home and that there were some issues over which they had more responsibility than the children. We were beginning to separate the parents from the children more clearly. This is often called 'restructuring'.

* * *

□□(a) Summary: what the workers did

1 The workers maintained the system boundaries by not starting before father arrived.

2 They followed up the homework task they had left with the family by asking to see the chart upon which family members were supposed to write what they wanted from each other.

3 They expressed the effect of the family here-and-now behaviour upon themselves: flashes of anger began to fly in the room which had the effect of puzzling the workers.

4 They requested the help of the family members in getting over their puzzlement by asking about the history of the behaviour (anger) that had triggered their feeling (of puzzlement).

All these interventions may be seen as being influenced by insight oriented thinking.

5 They further enlisted the help of the parents in exploring the expression of anger in the family by asking to meet with the parents separately. This move may be seen as a structural one. The workers separated the parents from the children in order to carry the exploration of anger further.

□□ (b) How else could the situation have been handled?

1 The workers could have followed through the insight oriented direction, and continued the direction in which they were moving up to step (a)4 by offering some form of interpretation at step (a)5. For example, they could have said, 'So the earlier years were different. Something probably happened between those days and now. It seems safer to keep throwing anger at each other rather than tell us what this was.'

2 The workers could have maintained the behavioural line for which the homework task was offered. They could have ignored the expression of anger by family members; instead of responding to it, they could have continued to praise the members' ability to do the chart and convey warmth to each other.

3 The workers could have attempted to intensify the expression of anger in the family so that family members exhaust the wish to use it and start talking about 'the real issue'. For example, the workers could (if they felt sufficiently comfortable with this) say something like: 'You all sound rather angry round here, but frankly this is nothing compared to what families who really express their feelings show us. If you're going to be angry let's have it all out now', etc. This would have meant taking a strategic line.

□□ (c) Approaching the crucial focus: some basic issues

Workers often ask, 'Suppose I have arrived at a "focal hypothesis", how do I actually get the family itself to focus on it?' Of course, there is no single answer to this. The

Approaching the crucial focus.

actual way of approaching the crucial focus depends on the circumstances as much as on the worker's style. However, some events seem to be predictable. A good focal hypothesis is not only imaginative, it is also based on accurate observations of repeated sequences of family behaviour. It incorporates the fantasies, wishes, and values that the worker has elicited from the family (by her questions, the tasks she has offered, etc.) with patterns of behaviour which, according to her observation, maintain the family in a steady state. There is never a full certainty that the worker has got it right. The key test is the family's reactions when the worker begins to respond to elements of the focal hypothesis more than to other events. For example, during the third interview with the Baileys the workers gently began to focus the family around their anger by sharing with them the effect it had on themselves and asking whether this had always been going on.

Now, if the workers' comment had had no impact on the family there would have been no certainty that the workers had really begun to approach the crucial focus. However, the family promptly changed track and began to chart its history as requested by the workers.

There are many ways of approaching the crucial focus and this is only one of them. Furthermore, it is not always necessary for the whole focus to emerge. It is enough that, having made a hypothesis about the crucial focus, the workers wait for some of the disabling behaviours which perpetuate the problem to surface. In the case of the

Baileys the hypothesis was that: (a) anger, (b) sending out, and (c) the exclusion of father, were used in order to avoid coping with the memories of an event that had happened four years previously. So, there were three elements to watch out for and any one of them would have been an appropriate signal. In the event, anger surfaced in the here-and-now of the session first. Accordingly, when anger erupted with no apparent reason the workers took it as a cue that it was time to test their focal hypothesis.

The test is a change in the steady state (anger, in the Bailey case) – suddenly there is attentive silence, or laughter, or embarrassment – something new is in the air. If this happens the worker can go ahead according to plan. It is quite surprising how, in spite of kicking and shouting, we all long for some truths, however painful, to be brought out in the open and dealt with safely. A good focal hypothesis meets this need in family members and will be accepted when it is accurate, especially if they feel the worker is on the family side.

Of course, we do not always get it right. When we do not have an impact on the family it is better to accept that it is us, the workers, who need to change. We might have got the focal hypothesis wrong, we might have failed to contract the work with the whole family, or we might have neglected some issues to do with warming up. When any of these reasons are identified it is better to go over them with the family again rather than assume that 'the family is too resistant to be helped'.

☐☐ (d) A different example related to approaching the crucial focus

The Ingram family, introduced in Chapter 6, included both parents and five daughters. The presenting problem was the middle daughter, Sally, who was truanting from school for no apparent social or educational reason that the school could identify. Sally refused to say anything about her truancy. After the workers offered the family the first interview they came up with the focal hypothesis that Sally's truancy was her way of drawing attention to her home situation. They had learned that none of the elder daughters helped in the home in spite of having left school and not looking for employment. Instead they were occupying themselves by having intense daily rows with Sally. The focal hypothesis was then enlarged to presume that the girls' 'idleness' was part of the Ingram family's inability to separate from each other as and when the daughters were growing up. (The initial focal hypothesis was elaborated further at a later stage, but is not covered in the present example.) The warm-up focus, offered to the family during the second interview, was for each of them to write what they hoped for themselves and what they wished from each other. This they accomplished enthusiastically, and the workers returned for the third interview to find the chart with the suggestions still hanging on the living room wall. There was cheerfulness in the air but, as expected, Sally was not part of it. In this case the workers felt that it might be possible to be quite direct in reaching for the crucial focus. They shared their pleasure at the good feelings around, and then said that 'naturally' none of these wishes was going to come true, because if any did mum would not feel as needed and the last thing the girls wanted was for her to feel she was not the super-mum she had always wanted to be. Also, the mother, because she loved her girls so much, would be just too worried if each went ahead and pursued what she really wanted to achieve on her own. The reaction was silence. Mrs Ingram blushed a little. Then one of the eldest daughters said to the workers, 'Are you saying that we are little girls?' The workers replied that they did not say they *were* little girls, but that the girls were doing their best to behave like that in order to remind mum how important she was and always would be for them. The eldest girls did not like the workers for this sort of frankness, but in the following interview they were told that the rows at home had diminished and each of the eldest daughters had begun to pursue what she had said she wanted for herself. Mrs Ingram was actually happier too.

This was a very prompt and some may say aggressive testing of the focal hypothesis. The workers drew some anger on themselves (and away from Sally?) by being so direct, which is not always a useful thing to do. The workers could not say exactly what led them to feel that they had permission to behave like this, and even much later were not sure it was the best intervention. However, in the event, it did confirm the focal hypothesis by the girls' behaviour change after the interview.

□□ **(e) Activities for further learning**

1 **Read further and reflect on the following interventions:**

   (a) **Making boundaries (Minuchin and Fishman 1981: 146–60)**
   (b) **Self disclosure as feedback (Egan 1975; 130–81)**
   (c) **Restructuring (Minuchin and Fishman 1981: 142–45).**

2 **Try to remember an issue that you have struggled over and felt quite blocked with in the past.**
3 **What do you remember from that time; what did you dread most, that is what was your 'dreaded calamity'?**
4 **How did you behave and what part of your cover-up behaviour (withdrawal, irritability) do you think others could see?**
5 **If you had a person to help you (such as a sensitive parent), what could he/she have picked-up from your cover-up behaviour and how would he/she have reacted to it?**
6 **Role-play the situation.**

Now, let us continue the workers' account of working with the Bailey family.

5 April

Couple's interview 1: WORKING THROUGH THE CRUCIAL FOCUS – *connecting the present to the past*

Sometimes the children in a family will not allow their parents to sort out their own

business. The beginning of this planned interview was taken up by Di's refusal to leave the room. Upon our insistence that this was the parents' meeting, she departed. Later on, Mary burst into the room demanding money to go to the cinema. We incorporated her entry into our work with the parents, but subsequently we could clearly hear her, through the half open door, wandering around in the kitchen.

When we were left alone with the parents we raised the subject of the children's constant expression of anger. The parents gave the stereotyped replies of children resenting being told what to do and being spoilt. It became clear to us that we would have to be more direct. We said that frankly we were rather horrified by the intensity of the anger. Was there anything else that could be connected to it? There was no reply. We plunged in and said that we should be honest and share with the Baileys that we knew from our records that four years ago Mrs Bailey left home for a while. We wondered what that had been about? Here came the crunch. Mrs Bailey appeared agitated, fidgeting and swinging her foot backwards and forwards. Her discomfort was acknowledged. She then retorted angrily that the matter was private and irrelevant to our concern. Mr Bailey said that he had forgotten about it all . . . We said that we felt stuck; there was nowhere to go from here. It should be made clear that a 'confrontation', which is what we offered, is not to be confused with accusations and abuse. We did not condemn the Baileys in any way. Instead we expressed the effect of the situation on ourselves and related it to what brought it about. The impasse was marked; we had to find a different way.

We returned to the line of how to help the children talk. What were they expressing beyond their words? One of us (Oded Manor) took Mary's role as an example, saying, 'If I were her, this is how I would have felt'. I knelt down and said, with feelings that quickly became quite real to me: 'Mum, help me. I feel so confused. I feel so many things at once. I don't know what I feel.' Mr Bailey said he wished Mary would have said this. Mrs Bailey said she did not know what to answer to this, and began to sob. She was hurt by her failure to get through to Mary. I acknowledged the hurt. I then suggested that we found ways for Mrs Bailey to get through to Mary. I took up the incident that had happened half an hour before. Mary had burst into the room shouting her request for money. How could Mrs Bailey respond to that? I suggested that we tried it out there and then, through a role play. My co-therapist assumed Mary's role and burst into the room. She needed a dry run to master Mary's vehemence, but soon got it right. Mrs Bailey was asked to respond. She began to put forward questions, that, as usual with adolescents, did not lead anywhere. We repeated the episode a number of times until Mrs Bailey was able to substitute statements for her questions. Our coaching of Mrs Bailey, as it were, in offering Mary openings for more real conversation made sense to the couple. They agreed to try to do this with the children during the following week.

As we left we thought that if they did help the children to open up, the past conflict might well be discussed privately and in their own time. We did not know that Mary was about to do something that would drastically speed up communication.

□□ (a) Summary: what the workers did

1 The workers maintained the boundaries around the sub-system of the parents as

separate from the children by insisting that they talked with the parents on their own.

2 They used confrontation to let the parents know of their feelings and shared with them hitherto undisclosed knowledge that the workers had of the family.

3 Faced with an impasse, the workers resorted to role taking while focusing on 'how to understand the children'.

4 They used role rehearsal to help mother talk to her daughter.

□□ **(b) How else could the situation have been handled?**

1 *Continuing to deepen confrontation*
Faced with the impasse, the workers did not have to change direction. Instead they could have pressed on with the parents' unwillingness to talk about what happened four years previously. They could have said for example, 'this is very stressful to us too. We are beginning to feel as if we are being put in your children's situation, and this makes us feel angry. If we were your children, it would make us feel as if you think we are so weak that we cannot face up to a simple truth. We don't believe in this kind of protection. It only confuses us. We're sure the truth will be easier to live with', etc.

2 *Adopting a behavioural line straight away*
Instead of asking what the children's anger was about, the workers could have plunged straight away into taking the children's role and practising with the parents alternative ways of reacting to their children's behaviour, as in steps (a)3 and (a)4.

3 *Adopting a structural line*
The workers could have attempted to alter the structure of the parents' involvement with their children by advising the father to take a more leading role in handling the children and encouraging the parents to spend more time together without the children.

□□ **(c) Working with an impasse: some basic issues**

In this interview the workers certainly hit an impasse. The wife refused to talk about the events that the workers thought were crucial to the resolution of the difficulties, and the husband 'forgot' about them. Facing and working with the impasse is, of course, crucial if change is to be achieved. Before we do that we need to understand what is entailed in this moment of paralysis that we call 'impasse', and what the options are for dealing with it constructively. There is no space here to discuss these issues fully, but a few thoughts may be in order.

Let us begin with what an 'impasse' is not. An impasse should not be confused with 'defensiveness'. The latter term is better kept to describe the client's apprehension about revealing too much too early to the worker. It may happen at any phase of the helping relationship. An 'impasse' is also not to be equated with 'lack of motivation'.

Regardless of the way one understands the concept of 'motivation' (and there is more than one way), an 'impasse' is not an indication that the client does not *want* to change; on the contrary, it is an ambivalent point when the wish for change clashes forcibly with the wish for continuity. We all carry with us these two conflicting wishes all the time. There are some moments when the clash between them is, therefore, inevitable. On the one hand we want to expand the possibilities open to us and overcome difficulties. On the other, we are attached to the memories, and the habits which are associated with being with loved people in the past. These memories nourish our sense of what we are and who we are going to become. They reassure us of the continuity of our ability to give our life some direction and meaning, and charge us with some sense of having a certain amount of power over the circumstances.

The question is what to do when faced with this ambivalence we call 'impasse' or 'resistance to change'?

You will find that practitioners differ in their strategies. Some, particularly if they are psychodynamically oriented, would focus on bringing the issue to consciousness by pointing out what is happening and virtually saying to the client that 'this has to do with your resistance to change'. Others, probably behaviourally oriented, would attempt to avoid reinforcing this behaviour by giving it as little attention as possible, and by focusing instead on smaller achievements that the client can make. The recent development within the strategic style is a third option. The strategic therapist seems to assume that 'resistance to change' is the essential component of therapy. The family is seen to resist the therapist since the therapist is the agent of change. Therefore, the therapist has to side-step the fight. She has to 'side with the resistance' by giving it positive connotations and even encourage the family to resist more strongly, that is amplify the resistance. The attraction of the strategic stance is in the full recognition that it gives to the ambivalent nature of the impasse. Why this strategy is valid is not yet as clear as the fact that it does seem to help in many impasse situations. In fact, it has been suggested that regardless of the therapists' theory, the amplification of previously disabling behaviour is part and parcel of the actual practice in many different psychotherapies (Haley 1963).

The workers with the Bailey family took a line that can be understood behaviourally. They let go of the issue of the past, and focused the couple on behaviours that would help them talk with their children. Their hope was that the family could share their past later when more trusting and effective communication between parents and children evolved. Not unexpectedly, the family system reacted in a more complex fashion. Often the disabling behaviours are intensified exactly when the system reaches the point of a crucial change. Amplifying the difficulty that brought the family to seek help is a very common phenomenon at this stage. Indeed, we shall see that Mary acted to fulfil this need by committing an offence a few hours after the workers faced the impasse with her parents.

□□ (d) A different example related to working with the impasse

The following example highlights a specifically social work dilemma. The dilemma stems from working under the pressure of time set by other agencies. The Ingram family, mentioned in the previous commentary, included the two parents and five daughters. Sally, aged 15 years, was presented as the problem due to her unexplained refusal to attend school. There were four more daughters in the family. The eldest aged 19 years, another aged 16 who had left school, and two girls younger than Sally, aged 11 and 8 years. The workers learned that although the two eldest daughters were not seeking employment or looking for their own accommodation, they would not do a single chore at home. Shopping, cooking, and cleaning were all left to Mrs Ingram who also worked part time. The three eldest daughters used to spend their time at home having intense daily rows, with the eldest two uniting against Sally. The focal hypothesis was that Sally's truancy was her way of drawing attention to the situation at home, and that the girls' 'idleness' was related to the family's inability to separate as and when the daughters were growing up. This was further elaborated when it was found out that Sally had been singled out by her mother as the one who would achieve success academically. Indeed it had been known that Sally had done very well at primary school whereas the other daughters had had educational difficulties. This suggested that Sally's non-attendance was her way of communicating to her mother through an issue that mattered. She was protesting against mother's over-protection of the family on the one hand and the exception of herself on the other.

The workers had been taking mainly a strategic line with this family up to the fifth interview. Changes had begun to happen, with the eldest daughter finding a council flat and the second eldest finding a job. The rows at home began to decrease markedly. However, one point had not yet been tackled. Sally was still not going to school. Since an Interim Care Order had been made and the court had granted a period for family work that would expire within five weeks, time was not on the workers' side. During the fifth interview the workers tried to approach the relationship between Sally and her mother. They began with the workers taking the role of mother and daughter and speaking for them. This was firmly blocked by Sally who left the room hurriedly. It was clear that they had hit an impasse and a crucial one at that. The dilemma was whether to stay with the relationship or change tack: how long could the workers afford to stay with the impasse without the risk of Sally being taken to court with nothing being resolved in the family? Rightly or wrongly, the workers felt that they did not have the time necessary to continue the line of approving Sally's refusal to talk while her mother put pressure on her to do so. They changed to a behavioural approach by suggesting how the parents could build a programme that would help Sally return to school. In the event, Sally did begin to attend school just in time for the magistrate to be satisfied with her progress and adjourn the sentence *sine die*. However, the workers were left with the unease of knowing that the mother–daughter relationship had not been sorted out, and might erupt into another presenting problem at any time. Although some interventions may be more effective than others when long term issues are considered, we cannot ignore the fact that social workers who have to meet the requirements of the court cannot always be confident that they will be allowed the necessary time. They may have to be more pragmatic and achieve smaller changes first.

□□ (e) Activities for further learning

1 Read further about the following interventions and discuss them with your colleagues:

    (a) Confrontation (Egan 1975: 156–72)
    (b) Role taking (Blatner 1973; Corsini 1966)
    (c) Role-play (Corsini 1966)
    (d) Modelling (Corsini 1966: 84–103).

2 Go over one piece of work you have carried out which included an impasse:

    (a) Clarify to yourself at what point the impasse emerged, making sure you are examining an impasse as defined in this book.
    (b) Role-play a psychodynamically oriented response to that impasse.
    (c) Role-play a behavioural alternative to dealing with that impasse.
    (d) Role-play the 'reframing' of the family behaviour in such a way as to confirm good reasons for leaving things as they are at the point of that impasse (that is rehearse a strategic response).

Now it is time to return to the workers' handling of the crucial focus with the Bailey family.

*   *   *

Events between interviews: MEDIATING BETWEEN MARY AND OTHER AGENCIES

On the evening after we saw Mr and Mrs Bailey, Mary broke into a flat on the estate. The flat-owner suspected Mary, found her with a friend, and stated that the perfume Mary was wearing was definitely the one used by her. Mary admitted it all straightaway, went to the police station and then began to shout and swear at everybody present. Mr Bailey was called to the station. He said that he could not cope with Mary. The police then issued a Place of Safety Order for eight days and placed Mary in the local assessment centre. As is customary, we were notified.

The following afternoon there was a telephone call from Miss Cole, the EWO involved. During her regular visit to the Baileys, Mrs Bailey had suddenly burst into tears. She told Miss Cole about serious marital difficulties saying that she realized they would have to be brought into the open. She asked Miss Cole not to mention the details to us before she had discussed the matter with her husband. Miss Cole urged Mrs Bailey to bring all this up in our next interview. We thanked Miss Cole for her good judgement and did not enquire further. Miss Cole also said that Di had returned to school recently with no difficulty, so that court action was no longer necessary.

The legal position regarding Mary's offence had to be clarified before we could continue our work, so we contacted the Juvenile Bureau. They explained that the flat-owner would not make a written statement about the offence, but was eager to explain to the Bench why Mary should be 'put away'. Consequently the Juvenile Bureau had to decide whether to make the charge themselves. They wanted to hear our opinion, and the nature of our involvement was explained to them in very broad terms. The officer concerned was adamant that a full case conference should be held, to which we willingly agreed but asked for some time to allow us to see Mary and her parents again. It was agreed that a case conference would be held three days later.

Our aim was to achieve a change in the way the parents handled Mary on this occasion. Specifically, instead of reprimanding her we wanted to see them make a different response, opening up some of the other issues that were involved. We contacted the assessment centre. Mary was said to have settled quickly there and to be very co-operative. We stated that we would like to hold a family interview at the centre the following day. The head of the centre sounded pleased and offered us any help we might need. We contacted Mr and Mrs Bailey and explained the whole situation including the interview we planned to hold at the assessment centre. The couple agreed to meet us beforehand and then travel together to the centre.

□□(c) The use of statutory powers in the mid-phase of work: some basic issues

In Chapter 6 we discussed how important it is for family workers to be honest about their views and the restrictions that are put upon them in regard to removing children from their families. Often the pressure for workers to take statutory action becomes very hard to resist again in the mid-phase of the work. It usually comes up as we approach the crucial focus, between the third and the fifth sessions, as happened with the Bailey family. As work gets to a point where change is imminent, tension is created and there is a rise in anxiety in everyone concerned – the family, the workers, and the other agencies. Everyone becomes uncertain about the process and the effectiveness of the work being done with the family.

As a result of this tension and anxiety a number of things can happen:

- The family turn back to their old ways and insist that 'the therapy' is unsuccessful and 'action' must be taken.
- A member of the family shows acute mental or physical symptoms.
- A member of the family leaves or is pushed out.

In all these circumstances the social services are often called upon to take statutory action. In spite of the previous hard work done in getting co-operation from colleagues, and however much the workers have kept them in the picture, to some 'therapy' is seen as ineffective and the risks too great to continue at this point. It cannot be emphasized strongly enough how difficult it is for the workers not to be paralysed by their anxieties into accepting the message that the therapy is not working; the risks are too great. However, some alternative options have been found useful.

HOLDING THE LINE

The workers can hold firmly to their plan, sometimes against advice, believing the panic to be an indication of imminent change. In the following example two workers resisted the pressure to remove Janice from home although both admitted to each other that faced with that pressure on their own they would probably have made arrangements for reception into care.

EXAMPLE

Janice O: a bridge across a split family

Janice was 15 years old, the youngest of a white family of four girls, whose parents had been separated for some years. She became pregnant by her black boyfriend. Her mother, who was very racially prejudiced, refused to allow her daughter to remain at home and pressurized for Janice to be received into care. The Education Department was equally concerned about her truancy and poor attainment at school. The social workers believed mother to be serious in her threat and were anxious about the possible risk to the girl if she were thrown out of home. However, they were convinced that she should remain the responsibility of her family. The social workers took a firm line, refusing to accept the child into care, but at the same time offering regular family sessions to all family members and saying that they would make arrangements for a mother and baby home if necessary at a later stage in the pregnancy. During the sessions, Janice's behaviour was re-framed as bridging the gap in this split family. One sister, who was living with her husband (also black) and her father (a very sick man), took the same view of the problem as the social workers and gave Janice temporary shelter. This gave Janice a first and only chance to be close to her father, who died very shortly afterwards. The death provided an opportunity for reconciliation for the whole family. Mother was genuinely helpful about the funeral arrangements, and showed her own sadness. Janice decided to have an abortion, returned home to her mother and later to school where she did well. At the follow-up three months later she had left school and was in regular employment.

USING LEGAL POWERS FOR TRANSFORMATION

There comes a point when a child may need the experience of containment while parents need a break from acute anxiety. However, that should not necessarily mean complete family breakdown. We believe that parents must be involved in family sessions concurrently with statutory action. In the following example statutory powers were used to stabilize the family situation, and then to shift 'the problem' back into the family domain of responsibility.

EXAMPLE

Barbara L: from 'mad' through 'bad' to ordinary life

Barbara was 16 years old. She had twice been admitted to mental hospital; she was diagnosed as psychotic. She had been very disruptive at home and occasionally violent, and she believed that she was pregnant by the god Ru. She rocked her imaginary baby constantly. There were veiled suggestions of incest. Her parents were at the end of their tether and unable to help her because they were frightened of her behaviour, but they still felt some responsibility for her difficulties. She and her father had been very close. There was serious concern about such a young girl being admitted to a mental hospital and the social worker negotiated with a helpful psychiatrist about the possibility of re-framing her behaviour as 'disobedient', that is, bad rather than mad. At her next outburst a Place of Safety was taken, followed by an Interim Care Order, and although her behaviour remained bizarre and she assaulted a police officer, she was placed at a children's home with education (CHE) for assessment. Within this strict regime she settled quickly and her behaviour became acceptable within a week. She remained very challenging of authority and needed firm handling. Family sessions took place on a weekly basis. Her parents ceased to feel frightened of her and began, with help, to react more firmly towards her. Communication improved and they began to enjoy each other's company.

At the court hearing, social workers recommended a six-month Supervision Order (an unusually short period for supervision), which was granted. Family sessions continued at home and after Barbara's initial testing-out of bizarre behaviour, the improvements continued. Towards the end of the six months the family's secret (incest with paternal grandfather) was discussed. However, this never became the central focus of the work, which was always on the present behaviour and communication in the family rather than past traumas. At follow-up after three months the family remained settled and the girl was in employment.

FOLLOWING THE RESISTANCE

There are times when the acting-out behaviour is such that it is not possible to do other than take the statutory action which is being demanded, but this does not have to be the end of family work. Allowing the family to resort to statutory means which protect them, can be seen as a temporary measure that is followed by more family work.

EXAMPLE

Mrs Burton: action speaks louder than words

There were serious marital problems between Mr and Mrs Burton, and a number of agencies were rather concerned about the care of the children. Soon after family work started, Mr Burton left the home. Mrs Burton reacted to this by exhibiting some very bizarre behaviour: she held the baby over the balcony rail threatening to drop him; she refused to look after the flat or feed the family; and became mute. The night duty social worker was called out at crisis point and admitted Mrs Burton to a mental hospital. Mr Burton who had not moved out of the neighbourhood, came back to care for the children. A Non-Accidental Injury conference was called as a result of which the children were placed on the 'At Risk' register. As soon as Mrs Burton was admitted to mental hospital her behaviour became normal and as the psychiatrist could find nothing wrong with her she was discharged home. Mr Burton remained at home (which was presumably what Mrs Burton had meant to achieve) and family work was resumed. The children were eventually removed from the register. It can be seen in this example that the behaviour was so dangerous the local authority had to exercise power to protect the children from serious danger, but as soon as this was acted upon the resistance to change stopped and work could be resumed.

We think that in dealing with all these crises an important aspect was the support and advice of colleagues and co-workers. It cannot be over-emphasized how necessary this is. It is also very helpful to include in the support system at least one person in a senior position who is able to back up some of the risk-taking and to explain it to those in higher authority.

With these issues in mind, let us return now to see how statutory powers were used while working with the Baileys.

*　　*　　*

10 April, afternoon

Couple's interview 2: WORKING THROUGH THE CRUCIAL FOCUS – *truth about the past in preparation for the future*

Although the parents knew we wanted to use the time together for planning the evening interview with Mary, they took over first. Mr Bailey gazed at us intently when he said that he had now told each of the children that when they were young he was imprisoned a number of times. Previously it had been explained to them that he was working in a prison. We sustained eye contact and acknowledged that it must have been very hard to talk about such things and that we admired his openness. Mrs Bailey was then able to explain to us, still trembling a little, that four years ago she could not take the imprisonments anymore, so she left for a while. We shared some of the feelings and practical stress that a prisoner's wife has to go through, and then emphasized to the couple that they needed to talk to all the children together about these years. We explained that, unless they did this, no child would know what had been said to the other, and this would invite back-chat in the family, gossip, and room for fantasy. With some hesitation they agreed. We said that they were really making a tremendous effort and that we would offer our assistance if necessary. Less was discussed about the meeting with Mary and time was running out. We reiterated our need to know if Mary could return home and when, and briefly reminded the couple about the difference between putting questions to Mary and making open-ended statements. The journey to the Assessment Centre passed amicably.

*

10 April, evening

Parents and Mary at the assessment centre: WORKING THROUGH THE CRUCIAL FOCUS – *father and daughter learn to talk to each other*

We were already seated in a comfortable sitting room when Mary burst in, full of herself

and her work at the school attached to the centre. It was such a joy to see Mary cheerful for a change and we all joined in with her enthusiasm and praised her work at school. It was good to have a positive opening. Mary soon settled for a close and continuous conversation with her mother. The rest of us were excluded. Mary began to talk about boyfriends and said that she did not know how to cope with them. We had been waiting for an opening like this. It was emphasized to Mary that the best person to ask was her father. This gave Mr Bailey the opportunity to say that he cared about Mary. He was asked to say this directly to Mary. He did, and Mary blushed. We continued with this 'restructuring'. It was suggested that perhaps Mrs Bailey could help Mary and her father talk more to each other. Mrs Bailey said that Mary had difficulties with that, she had always had. When asked about it, Mary said that she did not like her father shouting at her. Mr Bailey commented that his shouting came after Mary shouted first.

We suggested a 'contract'. If Mary shouts, Mr Bailey is to wait and remind her to speak calmly. Only then will he discuss her concerns with her. Mary looked pleased with that. It was suggested that Mrs Bailey should remind the two of them about the contract when they failed to adhere to it. Mr Bailey then talked further to Mary, explaining that he had been strict with her so that she would not get into trouble as he had. Mary listened attentively. We then said that we would be talking to the police the following day. If they agreed and Mary could shout less, she could return home after the eight days were over. The interview ended on this note and we left the assessment centre with the parents. Outside we questioned the parents about their plans for Mary. They said they wanted her back home. They felt things were beginning to change and that the placement was a good warning for her. When we pursued this they sounded confident and expressed themselves realistically and with some conviction. We said we would relay this to the police the following day, and would let the Baileys know of the result.

*   *   *

□□ **(a) Summary: what the workers did**

1 The workers brought the parents to the assessment centre in order to continue family work there.
2 The workers reinforced Mary's achievements at school work.
3 The workers involved father in relating to Mary directly.
4 The workers restructured the relationship by asking mother to 'help' father and daughter speak with each other.
5 The workers suggested a 'contract' that would facilitate more talk and less shouting between father and daughter.
6 The workers continued to mediate between the family and the police.

□□ **(b) How else could the situation have been handled?**

1 The workers could have brought the whole family, rather than the parents only, to the assessment centre, and conducted a full family session there.

2 The workers could have offered the family an opportunity to talk more about issues relating to sexuality in the session.

3 The workers could have explored whether Mary's role in the family reflected marital difficulties that should have been taken up with the parents alone.

□□ (c) The use of analogies during a therapeutic crisis: some basic issues

Breaking through the impasse often leads into the experience of a 'crisis' of some sort. Once the holding on to painful issues and exploding inwardly is given up, this 'implosive' stance turns into an explosion. During the explosive phase the family often intensify the presenting problem, and with it the patterns of behaviour they used in order to cope with their major difficulty. In the case of the Baileys we can see that they have now passed through the holding-in 'implosive' stance – that of refusing to talk to the workers about the events that happened four years previously. They are now going through the explosive stage. True to the nature of such a 'crisis', events are unfolding which repeat the 'game of sending out'. Mary did something dramatic in a fashion that guaranteed she was 'sent out' to the assessment centre. Father was excluded yet again from an opportunity to help her.

Often one family member commits an offence right in the middle of family work and involves other agencies. However, this should not lead the workers to feel that they have lost their hold of the family system. Rather, the workers should continue to be good system analysts and to this add being shrewd system *analogists*. Workers can learn to understand and anticipate the repetition of the presenting problem in the middle of family work as a reflection of the way the family system resists change. This often happens in the middle of a time-limited piece of work and is experienced as a crisis for both the family and the workers themselves. However, such a crisis is potentially therapeutic. It is as if the family are dramatizing their difficulties for the workers to see them on a large screen in detail. The workers then have the opportunity to react in ways that facilitate a resolution. In order to do so the workers' reaction to the crisis has to be an analogy of the potential solution. Without necessarily putting this into words the workers can convey an important message to the family. By their analogy they may say to them, 'you may choose to enlarge the screen for us, but small or large as the screen may be, the script *we* follow will be our own'. Let us take the Baileys as an example: the initial 'small screen' was the family home. The workers hypothesized that 'the script' (the systemic move) which would help would be for the family to get together in times of stress rather than send somebody out. Mary's action prompted a crisis that enlarged the screen. It now included the police and the assessment centre. So, the workers could not proceed with the original systemic move. The small screen (home) was lost for a while. However, they found a way of prompting an equivalent systemic move (in this case, bringing the family together) on the large screen (the assessment centre), so nothing was lost. As a result the family did make the necessary move although initially in a context different from their home. Change was first achieved by an analogy.

Any systemic move (process) can be projected into almost any context (or content) by the use of an appropriate analogy. Children create analogies all the time: they make up the most fantastic situation with fairies, demons, and all (their context), but then argue ferociously about the 'right' rules for it (the process), so that fairness and enjoyment are ensured. Indeed, it seems that it is not so much the fairies and demons they are learning about as the ways these figures might or ought to behave (that is the process that might or ought to occur). Whether these are analogies of their own internal world or of the interactions in their families or both, is of great interest to child psychotherapists. We also know that the enlarged context of fantasies children create can frighten them and may cause them to stop the play. We suggest that likewise, the enlarged screen that the family creates during the therapeutic crisis can frighten many experienced and competent adults. But adults should not stop 'the play'. On the contrary, they should recognize it as a strategy designed to frighten them with demons of some sort and persevere with the systemic move they think may help, projecting it into the newly created scene all the same.

An analogy is the projection of the same systemic move (process) into different contexts: father listening to son (the systemic move) can be projected into many different contexts – it can happen while fishing or over the family meal, or it may be first attempted more remotely when 'the king' listens to 'the prince'.

Analogies can also be created in many different ways. In Chapter 8 we discussed the use of images and metaphors as an aid in enabling the phase of warming up. These may be called 'symbolic analogies'.

During the therapeutic crisis families often create a context in which social workers, by virtue of their statutory brief, have to act. Verbal symbolic responses may not be enough. Action, if planned as an analogy of the potential solution, can not only keep social workers within their statutory brief, but even more importantly, may actually have far greater impact on the family.

Minuchin is a notable pioneer of what may be called 'structural analogies' in his in-session work with chaotic families who are more responsive to action than to words (Minuchin 1974: Chapter 8). We are suggesting here that social workers in local authority offices will benefit a great deal from extending structural analogies to the networks (formal as well as informal ones) into which the family chooses to import its behaviour.

There is, of course, still much to be learned about the creation of structural analogies between families and the networks they involve. Tentatively indeed, let us examine how we think when designing structural analogies. By 'structure' we mean the use of power and the alliances in the family: who has the influence to direct others (power) and who sides with whom over what issue (alliance). We then keep asking ourselves a number of questions.

While assessing the family structure we ask:

(a) Exactly who has the power, and who sides with whom in relation to what issues?

For example, in the Bailey family Mary had the power over the issue of what to do when in distress and mother sided with her.

(b) Who will need to do what for this structure (power and alliance) to change?

Again, with the Bailey family, it was father who would have had to become more involved and mother to support him more.
When the therapeutic crisis occurs, we ask:

(c) Who are the new 'players' and what role does each occupy to perpetuate the family game?

With the Baileys, the new players were the police and the staff of the assessment centre. Their roles were very much to be the punitive 'baddies' who keep family members distant from each other.
It is then a matter of identifying:

(d) Who will *now* need to do what for this structure to change all the same?

The workers with the Bailey family decided to 'neutralize' the new players by buying time with the police and achieving co-operation from the assessment centre which allowed them to carry on with their initial plan from the home (as in (b)) into the extended context of the centre.

□□ (d) A different example related to the use of analogies

The worker can, of course, use her imagination to combine different types of analogies as they serve a particular purpose. Here is an example: the family consisted of mother, her two adolescent boys and a girl. The parents had divorced and father's contact with the children had been sporadic and unpredictable. The presenting problem was the eldest son, Don aged 15 years, who either truanted from school or, when there, was repeatedly involved in fights with other boys. Work with the family seemed to progress quite well over the first four sessions with mother drawing boundaries more clearly and learning to praise the children's achievements. Then, not surprisingly, as life became easier there was a crisis. Mother phoned the worker to say that Don was involved in stealing sweets from a shop and was cautioned by the police. Mother felt alarmed as well as humiliated by the incident. The workers discussed this before turning up to the scheduled family session. It seemed to them that a lad of fifteen who stole sweets might be trying to say something to his family through action rather than words. In the family context stealing had a shameful but also somewhat heroic aura around it. Also, it seemed as though when things improved someone needed to show the workers how 'bad' they could get. The workers decided to side-track the moral punitive reaction Don might have expected from social workers yet not ignore the message. Instead, they would try to enter Don's shoes and find out what was the message behind his stealing. They started the session by saying that they wanted Don to help them understand the stealing incident. The male worker offered to pretend he was him and the female worker began to draw out from Don how it all happened step-by-step, which the male worker enacted in the family living room as faithfully as he could. As the male worker was going through the act he also imagined he was Don, and kept saying whatever feelings were rising in him – the fear, the excitement, what'd Mum do, what'd Dad say? etc. Don became intensely involved and insisted that the worker played his actions exactly as they had occurred. He corrected the worker's feelings and added his own as they went along. The female worker, who had been observing him, said later that he looked deeply moved and close to tears. The workers ended the session by expressing appreciation of Don's 'help' and saying they wanted to think a bit more about it all. In their discussion the female worker suggested that Don's intense involvement conveyed to her a feeling that indeed there was something unsaid in the family which he was struggling to let out. The workers decided to have a session with mother alone where it transpired that she felt intolerably guilty for having to put the two eldest sons into Council care when they were young and suspected they bore a grudge against her for that. The fact that their Reception Into Care was a consequence of the marital difficulties prior to the divorce was unknown to them. The workers helped mother relieve her guilt and then had another family session when the whole issue was raised by her and discussed with the children to very good effect.

When in the middle of family work a family member commits an offence, the act is very likely to be a message about the family relationship. The offence can be taken as a message and re-enacted in the presence of the whole family by the worker. Such a mix of an 'active' (the worker does it herself but in a different way) and an 'enactive' analogy (the worker does not talk about the meaning of the offence but acts it) has a number of advantages: it channels the communication act (that is the offence) back into the family system, it shows the family members a different mode of communicating the message (by the worker disclosing her feelings during the enactment) and it creates a feeling of 'neutrality' that offers safety and enables wider exploration of the message.

□□ **(e) Activities for further learning**

1 **Read further about the following interventions and discuss them with your colleagues:**

    (a) **Empathy (Egan 1975: 76–89 and 143–50)**
    (b) **Making contracts (Patterson 1971; Peine and Howarth 1975)**
    (c) **Restructuring (Minuchin and Fishman 1981: 142–45).**

2 **Now, let us go back to the Bailey family and assume that on 6 April, the day after couple's interview 1, instead of Mary breaking into the neighbour's flat, her brother Don, aged 12 years, was suspended from school. It was alleged by school that he physically assaulted his female teacher and was abusive to her 'for no apparent reason'.**

    (a) **Devise an intervention that includes a structural analogy.**
    (b) **Devise an intervention that includes an enactive analogy.**
    (c) **Devise an intervention that includes a symbolic analogy.**

Meanwhile 'action' continued for the Bailey family to which we shall now return.

* * *

. . . soft or hard?

11 April

Case conference with juvenile bureau: IS THIS SOCIAL WORKER SOFT OR HARD?

The case conference with representatives of the Juvenile Bureau was held as arranged. One of us (Oded Manor) described in very general terms what we were offering and put Mary's offence in the context of family dynamics without mentioning personal details. I explained that much of our work had been to enable Mary to see that her father cared for her, so she need not resort to obtaining material things or continually expressing anger. From this point of view removing Mary from home now could be seen by her as confirming her suspicion of her father's lack of concern for her. The officer-in-charge saw this point, but also seemed to assume that I meant that he should take a 'soft line'

approach. He offered to do nothing since the parents said they could handle Mary now. My next response surprised him a little. I said that while I could not see that we had grounds to recommend that Mary should be taken into care, adolescents must receive some reaction for whatever they do. His eyebrows rose and he seemed lost. However, when I explained my position further he agreed to caution Mary. It was tempting to start a discussion of the issue of punishment as deterrent as compared to punishment as a means for learning, but the case conference had to end.

*

12 April

Fourth family interview: WORKING THROUGH THE CRUCIAL FOCUS – *family members share their secrets*

By this time Mary had been returned home, so we had the whole family together again. We started this interview by talking about Di and how pleased we were that, as Miss Cole had told us, she was doing well at school. It was a good sign to hear the parents praising her behaviour at home without any prompting from us. We then repeated the facts about Mary's situation and explained the meaning of a police caution in the presence of the whole family. We also reminded them that the CGU were still intending to complete their assessment of Mary's schooling. We then gave the parents an opening by saying to the children, 'There are other things that your parents may want to talk to you about'. There was a minute's gap. Mr Bailey started quietly:

'I want to tell you some things about the earlier years,' he said.
Tony retorted, 'We know it.'
Mr Bailey: 'What do you know?'
Tony: 'You were in the nick.'
Di: 'Yea, we know, you were in the nick.'
Mr Bailey: 'How do you know?'
Tony: 'Nan told us.'
Mr Bailey (exchanging quick glances with his wife): 'Your Mum?'

The atmosphere was tense and angry. Here were two parents trying to protect their children from some painful facts without knowing that the maternal grandmother had pulled the carpet from under their feet long ago. This invited a return to accusations. Accusations would kill communication now. We needed to side-track the grandmother's behaviour. We addressed the children saying something like, 'Your father is trying to do something very courageous', and saying to Mr Bailey, 'We really respect you tremendously for what you are doing, let's carry on'. Mr Bailey was then able to go through the facts of the early years with a calm and dignity that was very impressive. He also mentioned Mrs Bailey leaving the family with another man. Mrs Bailey confirmed this. Yes, the children remembered standing outside the door in the evening waiting to see if she would come back. Di turned her back and began to cry. Tony looked straight into his mother's face and said tensely, 'You left'. He sounded accusatory again. To open up communication, the feeling behind this had to be aired. We said, 'You sound angry,

Tony'; 'Yes, I am' he replied. Mrs Bailey began to talk. She described how she had tried to dissuade Mr Bailey from offending, to no avail. She had to show him that she meant it. She said, 'It was horrible to leave you all like that, but it had to be done, and it's easier to leave with somebody else.' Mrs Bailey was choked, and began to cry heavily. It was then so important that one of us (the student co-therapist), who tended to adopt a fairly passive role in the interviews, was able to extend an expression of support to the family member currently in the most vulnerable position, on this occasion the mother.

Mary then said to me, 'Stop this, you bring Mum to tears'. Here was the other side of the coin – a child falsely protecting her parent from expressing feeling. Tears and hurt had to be interpreted differently, expressed in a different way, or 'reframed'. We attempted this by saying, 'Your mother has been crying about this for years because it hurts. It's only that she is letting you know about it now'. Mrs Bailey accepted this with silence. We continued to reframe: 'Nature gave us tears to cope with being hurt. If we don't use tears, there is only anger all the time'. One of us recalled our childhood and the fear of expressing strong feelings in the family. Children sometimes imagine that a calamity will occur once feelings are shared and that the family will fall apart, so they do things to prevent feelings from being expressed in the open. We needed to address that fear, and said, 'You don't need to protect each other so much. You're all very strong. I'm glad we are all here, taking our time. If we don't, there will be only anger here, as it has been up to now. The family will not go to pieces. It is growing stronger.'

It was important to let these precious moments be. There were silences. The parents added details from time to time. When people had time to absorb the experience partially, it seemed right to enable them to move on to a constructive resolution. This could be done by pointing to the positive side of what had happened. The previous crisis had resulted in the parents staying together and making considerable changes in their lives. We underlined this, and added that we admired the parents' strength and honesty. The children could make changes too. We talked about the change that Mary and her father decided to make. They described their 'contract'. We suggested that everybody should begin to remind everybody else not to answer back when anger was expressed, and instead, to wait till the other calmed down and then discuss the matter. The idea was accepted. In this way we avoided making Mary central in the family again and extended the change into the whole family system. No doubt they could all benefit from it. We also said that the parents had said they wanted some time on their own to go out and enjoy themselves. This was part of continuing the restructuring. There were problems about baby-sitting for Jim. Neither Tony nor Di nor Mary were forthcoming with help. We said that we would want to talk about this next time. We had all been through a lot that evening and felt exhausted yet hopeful.

* * *

□□(a) Summary: what the workers did

1 The workers praised Di's improvement at school, thus showing the parents how to reinforce positive behaviour and extend attention to members of the family other than Mary.

2 The workers relayed information from the police and the CGU so as to maintain the family links with other agencies.

3 The workers gave the session a direction by commenting that the parents had 'other things they wanted to talk to you about'.

4 The workers side-tracked the role of the maternal grandmother and focused the family on their here-and-now communication.

5 The workers attributed positive connotations to crying, i.e. reframed it.

6 The workers dispelled the family belief that sharing tears and distress will split them apart, and reassured them that such calamity was unreal and in fact the opposite was happening – the family was growing stronger.

7 The workers pointed out the positive side of the past crisis, i.e. the parents made changes in their life as a result of it.

8 The workers helped to channel the positives of the past into the present by suggesting that all family members adopt the new contract between father and Mary.

9 The workers continued to draw the boundaries between parents and children by mentioning the parents' wish to have some time out on their own.

□□ (b) How else could the situation have been handled?

This is not very easy to speculate at this stage because the scene has already been set so powerfully by previous events. However, two options come to mind:

1 The workers could have turned the family attention to the role of the maternal grandmother and enquired what role she played in the present.

2 When Tony said to his mum 'You left', the workers could have possibly given more space to exploring Tony's real role in the family.

□□ (c) Dealing with the unexpected: some basic issues

Unexpected events may erupt at any point during family work, but particularly during such a 'crunch' session. Different workers react to the unexpected differently, so only general principles can be discussed here. One principle is that of 'tracking with both hands'. Metaphorically speaking, the worker tries to keep both sides of herself – the thinking–planning–directing on the one hand, and the feeling–free–floating–reacting on the other – alive and well, with the hope that they both come to bear on the whole process. The worker may come to a family session with quite a clear scenario planned in advance, but find unexpected events that make that scenario irrelevant. If that is her judgement she may begin to 'track'. The process of 'tracking' or what some people call 'following the flow' is, of course, more intuitive than cognitive. However, experience suggests some guidelines. Here are questions that may cross the worker's mind as she follows the here-and-now of a family:

– How does this unexpected event affect me?

– Does it feel like a habitual behaviour charged with very little feeling?

— Does it throw me with its intensity of feelings; if so, what are these?
— Does it have an effect on the whole family system?
— Is it likely to stand in the way of dealing with any other issue?
— Is there something in this event from which the whole family can benefit?
— Does the event raise issues which the family is now ready to handle in a different and more constructive way?

If the worker can manage it (which is not always the case), she will respond only to events that are:

— charged appropriately,
— systemic,
— have potential for change now, and
— affect her in ways that leave her engaged warmly and undemandingly.

Therefore, events in which family members look largely uninterested, in which they are so intensely absorbed that they do not hear the worker (that is charged inappropriately), that do not affect the whole family (that is, are non-systemic), or that are such that the family cannot do anything about them, may not draw an immediate response. Events that do not involve the family may be ignored and the planned 'scenario' offered. If the events are over-charged the worker may acknowledge their importance and either suggest that 'we deal with this a bit later when we are all a bit more at ease with that', or the worker begins to 'hold it'. 'Holding it', is taking a back-seat and expressing empathy with whatever happens while trying to get as many family members as possible to express themselves as clearly as they can while describing what has happened. Such a holding operation not only lets the family members realize what is going on in more detail, it also gives the worker an opportunity to sense how all this affects her and where she may come in free of anxiety and less confused while hopefully seeing the wood for the trees (in other words the system that produced the event). This may enable her to intervene with regard to a family issue or pattern of behaviour that the family can take up now. One rule of thumb for such ambiguous moments is 'stay with your body'. If the worker feels tension in her body and her breathing is uneasy, she may assume that she has not yet connected well enough with the possibility for resolution and change. She should then wait longer before she intervenes at all. How she intervenes may vary considerably. The worker inclined to mix interventions of different sources will basically trust both hands. If the skill she has in one hand can 'do the job' and her other hand can offer it with ease and some spontaneity she will try an intervention. She should then be able to take a back-seat again and sense the reactions. If the intervention has had the desired effect she can follow it through, if it has not, she will revert back to 'holding' and ask family members what has happened now (or tell them how their reactions have affected her). Repeated cycles of 'holding', intervening, and the reactions to interventions usually get the process to the point where constructive work can be done.

□□ (d) A different example related to dealing with the unexpected

Let us take the Ingram family once again. The family comprised the two parents and five daughters. It became quite clear that their difficulties had to do with the eldest two daughters aged 19 and 16 years not being able to separate from the family due to mother's over-involvement and over-protection of the family. Work on releasing the eldest girl was progressing satisfactorily until the fourth interview. During the third interview the workers had met the parents on their own and had suggested that they adopt a behavioural line in preparing the girls to living independently. The parents had been very hesitant about such an orderly and planned approach, and had taken a long time to be convinced of its merits. In the end they agreed to meet with the whole family in two weeks time in order to talk about the details of programmes for each of the girls. The workers arrived for the fourth session to find only one girl and mother at home. Mother said that everybody else was busy helping the eldest daughter to move to a nearby council flat she had just been offered. On the one hand this was a very welcome move; and one the workers hoped for. On the other hand, the manner of going about the change did not allow the workers to see that it was enhancing further changes in the whole family system. It was an unexpected family move that threw the workers' planning out of the window. They could have stayed and offered mother and daughter separate attention, but this would have created a sub-system (mother–daughter) unconnected to the whole family. Their prime concern was the influence they had on the whole family system. Therefore, they shortened the session to a few minutes of exchanging some necessary information, agreed on the date of the next session, and left cordially.

□□ (e) Activities for further learning

1 **Read further about the following interventions and discuss them with your colleagues:**

    (a) **Communication training (Egan 1975: 156–72)**

    (b) **Reframing (Watzlawick, Weakland, and Fisch 1974: 92–109; Minuchin and Fishman 1981: 73–7)**

    (c) **Responding to the dreaded calamity (Ezriel 1950).**

2 **Here is a series of games to help you sensitize yourself to emotional flow and bodily tensions blocking it:**

    (a) **In a small group ask one member to volunteer a phrase, preferably one that includes an action (e.g. 'I like staring at you'). Ask all the members to stand up and attend to their own breathing for a few seconds and then to notice spots of tension in their bodies, and where they feel relaxed.**

Continued on next page

Continued from previous page

(b) Keeping this bodily awareness alive, ask another member to offer a different version of an action phrase and repeat it three times, then pause and discuss what she sensed in her body – more tension? less? where?

(c) Offer each member of the group (including yourself) a chance to do (b). Try to increase the pace as you go along; this makes the game more natural.

(d) Agree on homework task: each member is to concentrate on bodily tensions and relaxation while working in a real family (or individual) session. In your next meeting ask for as many examples of that experience as members can recollect.

The handling of the crucial focus with the Bailey family is over now and we shall see how the changes were consolidated in Chapter 10.

10 / CONSOLIDATING CHANGE

In this chapter, which refers largely to the fifth and sixth interviews with the Baileys, we look at extending and consolidating change in the family. However, since, in the work with the Baileys, this process was already started during the fourth session, we refer to relevant workers' activities from the end of that session in the summary and discussion of this chapter. Before that, let us continue the workers' story.

*　　*　　*

19 April

Fifth family interview: CONSOLIDATING CHANGES – *moving forward*

The atmosphere had eased considerably by this time. We did not feel that there was a need to deepen our involvement further. It was important to move on. In a light and warm manner we went over the new agreements again: how each would remind the other to stop shouting and start discussing matters calmly. The members took all this in good spirit. We raised Mr and Mrs Bailey's wish to have time on their own. We suggested that they describe to the children how this was important to them. It turned out that the parents had already had a night out the previous weekend. Tony had offered to babysit for Jim. We expressed our delight and in this way positively reinforced the change. It was an important part of 'restructuring'. Unless the parents had some life of their own which they could enjoy, they were likely to become over-involved with the children as a substitute. The children would then rebel and the family would be nearer to the old style of continuous clashes.

It was likely that the family would resort to some of their previous behaviour patterns. For one reason or another, people tend to go back to old habits. One way of helping with such 'relapse' is in fact to predict it. The relapse is then made part of the programme. Possible ways of overcoming it can be built in and discussed with the family in advance. Therefore we talked, without expressing too much concern, about 'ups and downs'. We said that we were aware that these might occur. The parents looked a little worried, but we said they were just another fact of life and discussed what they might do if and when further difficulties arose. We then mentioned that we had one more meeting together, and during this we wanted to hear how things would be left once our meetings had ceased. We began the 'countdown' later than usual because of the pace of the previous events.

*

26 April

Sixth family interview: CONSOLIDATING CHANGES – *tying up loose ends*

We commenced by asking how things had been going. Family members described more conversations between them. Mrs Bailey talked cheerfully about an all-night session that Mr Bailey had with the children, playing cards with them till six in the morning, while she had had a good night's sleep. Family members did look physically healthier. However, Don would not join us, but stayed in the corridor and later reluctantly moved to the corner of the living room. He was sending messages that all was still not well. In fact, why should it have been? Don's needs had not been aired. The situation felt real for us but very awkward. It was important to respond to it there and then. In this way we could show that other members had difficulties, not only Mary. It would help to make Mary less central and might prevent Don from starting a new set of 'problems' as a means for drawing attention to himself.

The difficulty was that Don would not speak, in spite of 'what's the matter with you Don?' approaches from all. One of us (Oded Manor) said, 'I don't really know what the matter is either but perhaps I could be Don for a moment'. I walked to his corner, adopted his bodily posture, and started to say whatever came to my mind as if I were Don. I felt there, in the corner, a sense of being left out, of being smaller than most other members, and expressed this. In this way I was taking Don's role and providing some words to express the feelings he might have experienced. Don then began to talk about Tony hitting him and calling him names. That was a good opening for reaching Tony too. We enquired about how Tony spent his free time. It became clear that he had no friends and was very bored. We mentioned a small group of young people of Tony's age and suggested that he might like to join them in doing things he enjoyed. Tony's eyes brightened up. Yes, he would like his name to be kept for when such a group started. We continued to pay attention to each of the other children by praising Di's progress. Only then did we raise Mary's situation briefly and relay that the CGU had been in touch with us. We added that we planned to meet with them prior to a decision about Mary's schooling being reached. We acknowledged that this was our last meeting and expressed our appreciation of the efforts that had been made by all. The parents returned words of thanks. We agreed on a follow-up meeting after six weeks.

17 May

Mary was cautioned by the police over the previous offence. They notified us about it.

□□ **(a) Summary: what the workers did**

FROM FOURTH FAMILY INTERVIEW:

1 The workers helped to channel the positives of the past into the present, by suggesting that all family members adopt the new contract between father and Mary.
2 The workers continued to draw the boundaries between the parents and children by mentioning the parents' wish to have some time on their own.

DURING THE FIFTH FAMILY INTERVIEW:

3 The workers encouraged the family to reiterate their agreement to try to discuss issues without shouting.
4 The workers reinforced the fact that Mr and Mrs Bailey had gone out on their own together positively, by expressing delight.
5 The workers introduced the possibility of relapse. By predicting this, the workers enabled the family members to discuss how they would deal with possible relapse, so this could be built in as part of the work.
6 The workers reminded the family that there was only one session left. They linked the present with the future by pointing out that the last session would be about how the family would function when the work was completed. This is known as 'countdown'.

DURING THE SIXTH FAMILY INTERVIEW:

7 The workers reviewed with the family how things had gone.
8 The male worker responded to Don's reluctance to participate in the discussion by taking his role in the here and now of the session.
9 The workers further decentralized Mary by following the role-taking with a discussion of Don and Tony's needs.
10 The workers began to connect the family to other agencies by relaying information from the CGU concerning Mary.
11 The workers rounded off the session by acknowledging that their involvement had now ended and expressing appreciation of the efforts made by all.

□□ **(b) How else could the situation have been handled?**

There are a number of possibilities here:

1 The workers could have extended the agreement by using Mrs Bailey's role as

arbitrator in the original agreement, and asking her and her husband to perform the same function for the other children as well as Mary. This would both extend the agreement to the whole family, and at the same time reinforce Mr and Mrs Bailey's parental authority.

2 Instead of extending the existing agreement between Mary and her father, the workers could have devised another agreement, based on similar principles, but applicable from the start to all the family members.

3 The workers could have left the agreement as it was, and moved straight on to concentrate on the restructuring process i.e. the issue of Mr and Mrs Bailey having time together.

□□ (c) Consolidation/extention of contracts: some basic issues

Now we move on to look at the design and implementation of contracts with which to extend change from a sub-system of the family (in the case of the Baileys, father and Mary) into the whole family system. For example, it is unlikely that Mary and her father would have kept their agreement to change their way of communicating for long if the rest of the family had continued to 'shout' as previously. In other words, a new behaviour would have been acquired, but overall the roles in the family would have remained unchanged, in that the family's perception of what was happening remained unaltered, and the family's 'rules' remained the same. The workers therefore chose to consolidate the work by extending the change that had occurred into the whole family system.

There are various ways of doing this, and the choice may depend, among other things, on the disabling strategy adopted by the family.

Here are examples of some ways to design extension agreements:

EXTENDING AN EXISTING AGREEMENT

This is usually appropriate when the whole system shares the disabling behaviour.

It is shown clearly in the case of the Bailey family. Although the communication between Mary and her father was used as a 'springboard' for a behaviour change, the workers were aware that all the family members took part in the shouting as a pattern of communication. For this reason, it was appropriate for the workers to extend that particular agreement to all the family members. As they all accepted the idea, we can assume that they had shared the workers' perception.

MAKING A NEW AGREEMENT

When the system is 'split', in that sub-groups adopt complementing disabling strategies, it is appropriate to design the agreement differently so that these strategies (such as, the nag–withdraw–nag pattern) are given-up.

For example, if the anger in the Bailey family was only expressed between Mr Bailey and Mary, while the other family members complemented the anger by withdrawing and becoming silent, the extension agreement used would not have been appropriate. In such a case, it could have been appropriate, for example, to make an agreement with the family whereby Mr Bailey and Mary together taught the other members of the family to express their feelings more openly. In this case, the change would have been extended to the whole system, while Mr Bailey and Mary's anger would be given a positive connotation. They would thus have a job to do together, which would disrupt the complementary interaction and reinforce the restructuring that had taken place.

ELABORATING THE RESTRUCTURING

When the system is 'enmeshed', a way of extending change to the whole system is to concentrate and develop the restructuring already started in previous sessions. In the case of the Baileys, if the family had not already organized for Mr and Mrs Bailey to go out together, the workers could have selected this as the major issue. They could then have made an agreement with the family giving each member a role in the task, 'helping' Mr and Mrs Bailey to go out together. This would serve the purpose of shifting the focus of work away from the distress between Mary and her father, and concentrating the family on a shared positive experience.

DEVELOPING A PREVIOUS INTERVENTION

Sometimes, after a hard and painful piece of work, the family and workers experience a 'plateau'. The energy level drops, and there is a danger of slipping back to the previous state of affairs. Experience shows that this may be due to the fact that some changes have not yet been worked through, or if the disabling behaviour has been entrenched over a long period of time, the system may be slow to absorb change. No doubt there are other reasons too, but it is important to distinguish between these and the possibility that the family is exhibiting resistance to change. In the latter case the workers will need to use different strategies, some of which we will be discussing later.

However, if the workers decide to stick with consolidation, it can be useful at this point to take the family back to a previous achievement in the work, usually during the warm-up phase. For example, they may return to a previous task that was achieved, or an analogy that the family were able to use constructively. It is then possible to reinforce the family's ability to change, and to develop an extending agreement from there. However, this time, the agreement would probably incorporate some material from the work done during the crucial phase too.

For example, in the work with the Baileys, had they got stuck in the fifth session it might have been appropriate for the workers to take the family back to the phase of work in the second family interview, when they expressed warmth and positive feelings towards each other. By reminding them how much they cared about each other, the workers could have either made an agreement with the family to deal with their anger more constructively, or enabled them to link that to the restructuring work, for example, arranging for the family to show their caring for each other by enabling Mr and Mrs Bailey to have an evening out together.

THE FINAL ASSESSMENT AND THE LAST MESSAGE

The workers, having attempted to extend the agreements to the whole system, need to assess the type of change that has taken place in the family. Usually this will be done during the following session. In particular, they need to assess whether the change that has occurred is of the first or second order.

First order change is partial change 'within the limits for behaviour that are already set' (Hoffman 1981). If the family's set of rules, the roles the members take in the family system, and the family's perceptions remain the same, the change that has taken place is of the first order. In the case of the Bailey family, the change in communication between Mary and her father was first order change (referred to earlier in the chapter). It may be that this type of change is what the workers and family were aiming for.

However, it may be that the workers were aiming for a comprehensive 'shift' in the system which would involve changes in the family's rules of behaviour, a re-assignment of the roles the members take, and changes in their very perception of what is happening in the family. This fundamental change is called second order change (see Chapter 2). Of course, first and second order changes are not mutually exclusive, and may well both be present simultaneously. It is useful for workers to refer to the original aims of the work to help them assess the type of change that has taken place.

Let us assume that the workers have made an agreement to extend change into the whole system, but the resultant change in the family has been partial, or first order change. In this case the workers are coming up against 'resistance' to change. Often the disabling strategy has a function without which the family become prey to the underlying fear or fantasy that the system needed to overcome. This was why the disabling strategy was developed in the first place. This is shown clearly in the case of the Bailey family. During couple interview 1 we see that they were resistant to change because of their underlying fear that the family would fall apart if a major change took place. In other words, the 'sending out', shouting, and abuse of Mr Bailey served the function of enabling the family to avoid dealing with the pain of the past and the concomitant fantasy of disintegration.

WAYS OF DEALING WITH RESISTANCE

There are various ways of dealing with resistance, depending on the workers' orientation. As was suggested in Chapter 9 (see p.94), a psychodynamically orientated worker might interpret the resistance to change as a means of bringing it to a conscious level. With the Bailey family, for example, this might entail sharing their fear of the family falling apart, in order to start working through their feelings.

If the worker was behaviourally orientated, she might divert the focus of work from this issue to another where the family are able to make some change, albeit to a smaller degree.

Another way in which change can be effected, sometimes in quite a dramatic way, is to take a strategic line. This entails not only accepting the family's defiance of the worker as resistance to change, but siding with the resistance and connoting positively. It may even be appropriate to give a message to the family suggesting that they resist change even more. For example, in the case of the Bailey family, suppose it became clear that in spite of the agreement about shouting that was intended to extend change into the whole family, the only change that had occurred was the original one between Mary and her father. This would have meant that Mary and her father were now able to discuss situations more calmly, but the rest of the family still did a good deal of shouting at each other. The workers are aware how frightening the underlying fear is to the family. The workers might say to the family 'We realize that change could be dangerous for the family at the moment, and you are absolutely right to continue as you are. By staying the same, you are all working hard at keeping the family together, which is what you all want'. If the workers have got the message right, resistance will dissolve and a shift to second order change will come about. This is known as a 'paradoxical injunction'.

If, on the other hand, the workers think that second order change has already come about after the extension agreement, the system has already overcome the resistance to change. In this case, it may be more appropriate for the workers to reinforce change in a straightforward way along behavioural lines. This is what the workers did with the Baileys in relation to the fact that Mr and Mrs Bailey had already had an evening out together. They did this by expressing delight at what had happened. This type of reinforcement increases the family's sense of achievement, and consolidates the changes they have made.

□□ (d) A different example related to consolidating change: the Kendall family

The Kendall family consisted of Mrs Kendall, aged 39, who was divorced from Mr Kendall, aged 43, and raising their children alone: Ashley (19), Frances (15), Debbie (13), and Michael (9).

THE REFERRAL

Frances Kendall was referred to the Social Services Department by the EWO because of truancy from school. When the EWO had visited the family at home, Mrs Kendall had said that Ashley and Frances argued all the time, and she was at her wits end. She said that Frances was beyond her control. There were several issues about which Mrs Kendall complained in relation to Frances: one was the time that Frances got in, not only from school but also when she went out in the evenings with her friends.

Crucial Focus

The Kendall family agreed to work, and during the first session it became clear that one of the major issues was Ashley's taking of Mr Kendall's place by assuming parental authority and controlling the younger children on Mrs Kendall's behalf. Mrs Kendall was therefore in a position of controlling the children through Ashley. The work during the crucial focus was aimed at restructuring the parental authority in the family so that Mrs Kendall could take control of the younger children herself, thereby freeing Ashley.

Agreement during the crucial focus

One of the agreements aimed at restructuring and made during the crucial focus of work was that Mrs Kendall would decide what time Frances should come home in the evenings, and that Mrs Kendall should decide how to reward or punish her accordingly.

Extension of agreement to the whole family system

After the above agreement had been achieved, the workers devised an agreement which affected all the family members. Previously, the family mentioned that Mrs Kendall expected Ashley to take the children shopping for their new school uniform, and Ashley had wanted to spend the time going out with his girlfriend. This was taken up now and an extension agreement was made whereby Mrs Kendall would take the three younger children shopping, and this would free Ashley to spend the day out that he had planned.

Reinforcement following a second order change

At the next session, it was established by the workers that this task had been completed successfully. Mrs Kendall had enjoyed using her experience to ensure that the children got the right clothes, and she had also taken them out for lunch afterwards. Ashley had enjoyed his day out at the coast with his girlfriend.

By using her parental authority Mrs Kendall had changed both the family rule that Ashley made decisions about the children, and roles that she and Ashley usually took in these situations. A change in perception was also made possible: everyone in the system could see that Mrs Kendall took over the parental authority, and Ashley went off to enjoy himself with no family responsibility. The change that had come about was second order change.

The workers were therefore able to take a behavioural line, praising this change. They could then move into a discussion about one of the main issues facing the family; this was the proposed move out of London and which of the family members would go. Previously, when this had been discussed during the crucial focus, there was a great degree of anger and pain related to it; Ashley did not want to go with the family but felt duty bound to do so. At the time, his mother was feeling desperate at the thought of trying to care for the other three children without Ashley, and there was a great deal of guilt and recrimination inherent in the discussion. Another issue which caused great difficulty for the family at that time was Frances's situation. Frances was also saying she did not want to move with her mother, and Mrs Kendall was wondering whether she would be able to care for Frances at home, or whether the girl would have to come into care.

After second order change was achieved, the workers were able to bring the discussion back to the question of the move. They were able to reinforce the fact that Mrs Kendall was able to control the children and enjoy spending time with them, and also that Ashley was able to feel freer to enjoy himself, and was therefore able to support his mother more when he was at home. After long discussion, it was agreed that Ashley would stay in London and that Mrs Kendall, Frances, Debbie, and Michael would take up the offer of the house in the country. Ashley would visit them regularly and the elder girls would be able to come and stay with him in London when they wished. The final session with the family was spent discussing the move, and praising (reinforcing) Mrs Kendall's achievements in having organized this, as well as her authority in terms of arranging it.

□□ (e) Activities for further learning

1 Read further about the following interventions and discuss them with your colleagues:

(a) Preparing for relapse (Haley 1976: 67–76)
(b) Countdown (Mann 1973).

2 Think of a family you are working with where:

(a) You have identified change in a part of the family system as a result of an initial agreement, but this has not yet been extended through the system.

(i) Clarify the initial agreement with a sub-section of the family system.
(ii) Devise an extension agreement to promote change in the whole system.

(b) You have already made an extension agreement, but where the family have resisted this, the only change identifiable is that of the first order.

(i) Clarify both the initial and extension agreements that were made with the family.
(ii) Discuss and think through with your colleagues what function the maintenance of the symptom serve for the family.
(iii) Plan a strategic intervention that connotes positively (describes as 'good') the family's current position.

(c) Second order change has come about.

(i) Devise a behavioural programme to reinforce that change.

11 / MAINTENANCE AND THE CLOSURE OF CASES

The discussion in this chapter follows the workers' last contact with the Bailey family when they came for a follow-up interview. We shall use the opportunity to comment here on the workers use of the network around the family, various ways of devising follow-up schedules, and the fashion in which cases are closed in a social services local authority office.

Before that, let us hear the workers' account of their last interview with the Baileys.

*   *   *

7 June

Follow-up interview: MAINTENANCE – *what has been changed?*

We began this interview by enquiring about family behaviour and interaction, although it was very obvious that the family atmosphere had changed altogether. It was warm, almost cosy, at times. Some members continued to look much healthier physically. We heard that there had been no problem about the children coming home on time at night. They had complied and anyhow were beginning to spend more time together at home, having conversations amongst themselves and playing cards. So, the problem that had led the parents to approach us seemed to have been resolved. In addition we learned that Mr and Mrs Bailey now arranged weekly nights out on their own. We could see that the parents were praising the children's positive behaviour now, instead of their old habit of paying attention to them only when trouble occurred. We expressed our joy at the achievements and used them to underline the family's strengths and abilities.

However, this was almost too good to be true. Often when people undergo such drastic change they become frightened, as if their sense of their own identity is threatened by too much change. We tried to allow for that too, and began to talk about 'ups and downs' again, saying that these might happen and asking what the members would do then. The parents described how one of them was sure to remember that they should not be drawn into mutual accusations – at least this was how they were helping each other now. Someone would remind the other to wait till the person who shouted calmed down. Nevertheless, we explored possible 'ups and downs' in some detail. In fact, we almost rehearsed possible relapses with the family. This could be of help to the parents to be prepared if and when they came. We then explained that the programme had ended and that if they needed further help, they could contact our duty office. This is important too. We need to make a clear break from the family. If we fail to do this, the family may not feel the need to pool their own coping resources, and instead may continue to rely on our help for as long as it is available.

Lastly, it remained for us to connect the internal changes that the Baileys had made, to their external environment.

*

CONNECTING INTERNAL FAMILY CHANGES TO THE EXTERNAL ENVIRONMENT

From the start we had been aware of Di's and Mary's involvement with a crowd of girls on the estate. Now this could be approached more positively. Miss Cole offered to liaise with our ITC and the troublesome crowd began to meet there with her on 17 June.

On 28 June a case conference was held by the CGU, at which we gave a general description of the changes that we had observed in the Bailey family. We emphasized that removing Mary to a boarding school would counteract our attempts to convince her that her parents loved her. However it became clear that Mary had created an impossible situation with her peers at her present school, and the decision was made to transfer her to a different local day school.

We felt that Tony also required attention. On 5 July he joined one of our adolescent groups where activities to his liking could be pursued and peer relationships developed through them.

*   *   *

□□ (a) Summary: what the workers did

1 The workers gathered accounts of the recent behaviour of all family members in order to assess what changes had occurred.
2 The workers praised the family for the changes that had been made.
3 The workers warned the family of 'life's up and downs' and rehearsed relapse with them.
4 The workers explained the end of the programme and checked that the family knew how to approach the Department should the need arise in the future.
5 The workers introduced the EWO to the staff of the ITC, where the 'girls' crowd' were later to meet.

6 The workers attended a case conference which linked their work with that of the CGU and the school.

7 The workers introduced Tony to an adolescent's group.

□□ (b) How else could the situation have been handled?

It is very difficult to suggest alternative ways of handling the situation so late in the process of work. Rather than being too speculative we shall use this space to discuss three important issues that arise at the very end of family work: *the use of networks, maintenance schedules,* and practical issues concerning *the closure of cases.*

□□ (c$_1$) Using the network: some basic issues

System theory suggests that the family is not only a system in its own right but also a sub-system in the larger scene which we call the network. The family's network includes all those individuals and groups with whom the family relates. Networks will have informal relationships such as those with a circle of friends and relatives (Hartman 1979) and formal ones of various agencies with whom family members negotiate about their needs. The latter may include employers, schools, the local CGU, or any organization where there are formalized ways for people to give and receive services. Here we shall concentrate on the formal network.

In Chapter 6 it was stressed that before the worker engages the family she must agree this with all the other agencies involved. Having harnessed them to the process of work she needs to continue to feed information into the network throughout. At the end of family work it is important that other agencies, who were asked to stay out of the picture for the time being, should be briefed about the progress which the family has made. This is important because part of the change in the family system is the family readiness to relate differently to organizations in the network. Yet these other agencies have not been directly involved and may not know this. We need to encourage them in new ways of relating to the family and vice versa. In Chapter 10 we described how change achieved by part of the family needs to be channelled into the whole family system. We now go further to say that change achieved by the whole family needs to be channelled into its wider network.

The worker who links the family with parts of its network does not do it without family approval and does not reveal intimate details of the work done with the family. It is best to ask family members what information they are prepared to let the worker share with other agencies and stick to this understanding as far as possible. Obviously, situations where risk to life or limb is involved must be discussed fully with relevant agencies. On the whole, it is surprising how seldom families insist on holding back if they see the purpose of sharing information with outsiders. This is helped if family members know that the worker is not a gossip. She will convey to others only those bits of information that concern observable behaviours (rather than attributed feelings); she will restrict her explanation to viable hypotheses supported by concrete evidence; and will refer only to matters that are of direct concern to the other agency.

It seems likely that our understanding of networks and how to work with them will continue to change and grow. Based on present knowledge it is difficult to endorse totally and unreservedly the recent wave of optimism about the caring potential of informal networks as a substitute for professional help (Hadley and McGrath 1980); although the attempt to enable the girls' crowd to find a better place than the street does go in this direction. We agree that much more accurate knowledge is necessary (Abrams 1980; Bayley 1981).

*

The approach we have described here may be called 'the linking model' and has its supporters in the US too (Maguire 1980; Swenson 1979). However, it should be stressed that some practitioners in the US have been far more adventurous. They do not believe in working with the nuclear family first and only then linking it back into its network. Instead they start right away to work with the whole network directly. Their work may culminate in a large group-meeting of up to forty people in the room, where the milkman, the vicar, a great aunt, or whoever else the family think may be helpful, all meet together in the process of 're-tribalization' (Speck and Attneave 1973; Reuveni 1979). This 're-tribalization model' should be of interest to many workers, particularly when the family is already widely involved with other sub-systems in the same locality. Our own experience is restricted to the linking model. It is worthwhile to look at another, rather extensive, example of it.

☐☐ (d₁) An example related to the use of networks

The Linden family was first mentioned at the end of Chapter 5 (see p.45). This example shows the usefulness of linking a number of formal and informal sub-systems to each other through the work done by the family workers. You will see how the family was connected to the IT service, to their girl's local friends, to contacts she had in the big city, to the Education Welfare system, and finally to a new school.

*

After the intensive family work with the Linden family was complete, the workers were unable to close the case, because Diana, the 12-year-old who had been in trouble, was still awaiting a place in a special school. There was concern that if she remained at home unoccupied during the day, she might begin to run wild once again. The family workers arranged for her to attend the ITC for day care, which included education. Her extraordinary energy was channelled very successfully by the IT workers and although difficult at times, she made good progress and became a leader in her group. She was a child who thrived on excitement, and the workers were well aware of the lure of the big city for her although she was currently obeying her parents and coming home at the time agreed in the evenings. In order to offer her a form of excitement which would help her to mature, a worker from the IT group and another social worker in the family workshop who specialized in work with adolescents, formed an evening group which

Figure 3 Network map: showing work with Diana Linden and her family

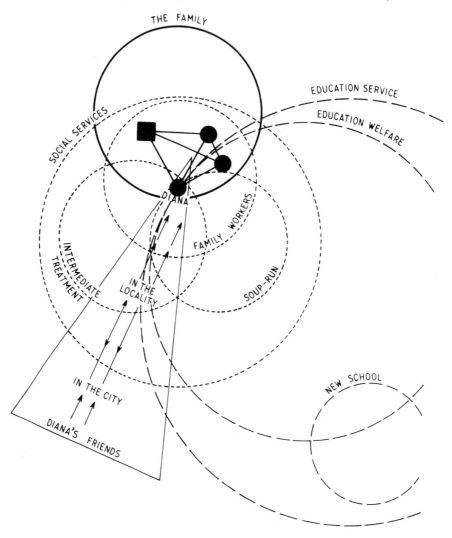

included Diana and a friend of hers. The group met in the late evening and went on a soup-run to the centre of the city, offering help to the homeless who were sleeping rough. As well as offering the girls a chance to consider the seamy side of city life, which Diana discussed thoughtfully, the workers became more familiar with the girls' previous experiences in the city and met some of their previous contacts there. This was a way of tracking the girls' 'secret' network which was acceptable to them because it happened spontaneously. The family workers kept in touch with their colleagues, who were working with Diana, and during their now infrequent visits to the family for maintenance sessions were able to review her continued progress and deal with minor problems of communication between the parents and others involved with her. This is an example of how the varied resources within a large department were used creatively together to maintain and encourage Diana's development. Meanwhile the family workers continued to liaise with the EWO, who had been a great support in their work, and who made plans with the new school about when to admit Diana. The case was closed at the point when Diana was settled in her new school.

□□ (c₂) Maintenance strategies: some basic issues

Whether you re-tribalize the network or merely help to link parts of it together, it is important to be aware of the forces in the family field that can work against change. Families, particularly in an urban industrial area, are exposed to many diverse influences – the media, the local culture, different age groups, different ethnic moral codes, etc. None of these is necessarily congruent with the others. It is not surprising then to find families reverting to disabling behaviours, unless firm guidelines are left with them as to how they can maintain and promote the changes they have achieved.

The social learning approach is very helpful in relation to this. It says that we all learn new ways of behaving all the time, and that behaviours that stick with us are those reinforced more often. It follows therefore, that there is no guarantee that improved performance, achieved *during* family work is going to be maintained *after* work ends, unless it is continuously reinforced. If the new behaviours are not experienced by family members as continuing to pay off they are abandoned, and other, possibly disabling ones, may be acquired instead. There are some simple and sound ways in which the worker can help the family maintain the changes, such as rehearsing with the family what to do when things go wrong again, leaving them tasks which give them practice in new behaviours, and teaching them to praise each other promptly (Goldstein and Kanfer 1979). Some of these are discussed in Chapter 10 but are equally applicable to this phase of work.

Devising these maintenance strategies is one aspect of the work that is fairly well documented. Timing them appropriately so that they fit the family's pace as well as satisfying the legal requirements binding social workers, has not yet been fully explored. When devising maintenance strategies, judgement about the frequency of follow-up interviews is important. Some families 'go slow' throughout their lives. They will absorb change more slowly. Such families should have the follow-up sessions spaced widely, with something like two or three months' interval between each session. More frequent sessions do not seem to achieve much and can encourage increased dependency on the worker. However, other families are 'fast movers'. Things happen constantly with never a dull moment. This difference of pace is neither 'better' nor 'worse' in itself (Olson, Sprenkle, and Russel 1979). All the worker needs to do is identify the family pace and match her own pace to it. Fast moving families should be offered more frequent follow-up sessions – perhaps with a four weeks' interval. If the frequency is lower, too much may happen between sessions that may sweep away even the best family work results.

You may begin to feel that these maintenance interviews require a lot of work after the intensive programme of family work has ended, and that this is not only contrary to the emphasis on separation from the family through the use of a time-limit, but also requires more time than social workers can afford. However, it may be necessary to offer only one follow-up session; this was true of the Baileys who were seen for six family interviews (plus a number of other interventions) over a period of six weeks, with one follow-up session six weeks later. Other families may need a larger number of follow-up interviews but they could be part of the total number of sessions agreed with the family. For example, the family may have been offered twelve sessions in the initial contract; eight of these sessions may be used during the intensive part of the work, spaced over a period of two months, and the remaining four sessions will be used for maintenance sessions with a month's gap between each. Alternatively, the maintenance period can be contracted separately at the end of a six session programme. Maintenance is usually done by agreeing on specific contracts among family members that serve to maintain achievements. These contracts can then be monitored by the workers during a number of follow-up sessions spaced in intervals of up to six months until they are satisfied that new behaviours have taken root in the family. Just to show that this is possible in a local authority office where statutory duties may be seen to interrupt a fixed schedule of follow-up, let us look at some data. *Figure 4* compares the rate of contact between workers and seven families who had been offered the time-limited contractual approach with seven other families with whom workers in the same office used the more established open-ended casework approach. All fourteen families had been assessed as high priority for allocation to a social worker and were quite similar to each other in most other respects. The graph shows that the families offered the open-ended approach involved their workers in what became known as 'the Yo-Yo game', in which the worker gives the family a lot of time and resolves one issue while waiting for the next storm to erupt when she will rush in again and spend the same amount of time on resolving another problem. This in-and-out chase can, as illustrated in this study, last for two years or more. You can also see that the pattern of contacts with the families to whom our contractual approach had been offered turned out to be different. After the first intensive period of fortnightly sessions the rate of contact with the families dropped consistently until it reached an average of 1.3 interviews every four months. The details of this study (Hurley and Manor 1977) cannot be fully presented here, but we hope that the main message is clear. Social workers in a local authority office can find a way out of the Yo-Yo game. They can build into the follow-up period strategies that the family members can adopt to overcome difficulties on their own while being visited periodically by the workers to monitor and if necessary modify these strategies. It should be emphasized that this also refers to families towards whom there are statutory obligations for the workers to remain in at least a monitoring role when Care or Supervision Orders have been made by a court. The solution in such cases is not to abandon the fixed schedules of maintenance sessions. Instead, it should be possible to negotiate with management how to adapt the requirements for monitoring such orders so that they both satisfy the court and support efforts to enhance the family's self-coping abilities.

Figure 4 The rate of contacts with families

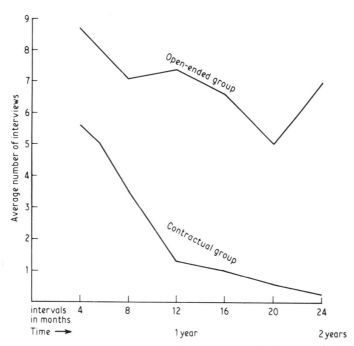

Average number of interviews every 4 months during 2 years for the Contractual group (N=7 families) and the Open-ended group (N=7 families).
Source: Hurley and Manor (1977).

□□ (d₂) An example related to maintenance strategies

Only partial success was achieved with a family of two parents and three school-age boys that resulted in Ken, the eldest aged 14, being made subject to a Care Order by the court and sent to a boarding school in East Anglia. The Care Order meant that we could not close the case and our assessment was that the boy needed to strengthen his relationship with his father and rebuild his self-esteem. We therefore negotiated with the senior social worker in charge that we should use the obligation to monitor the boy's development for family sessions twice a year at the boarding school. Every six months, over a period of two years, we arranged for both parents to go with us from London to East Anglia, meet the staff at the school, and talk with Ken about his achievements there. We deliberately adjusted the times so that father could come too and he never missed a session. When Ken was sixteen he returned home and quickly found a job, at which time we asked the court to discharge the Care Order.

□□ (c₃) Ending: some basic issues

There is little in family therapy literature about termination and even less about the relationship between worker and family at this time. It may be helpful to consider why. For those who have come to family work from a traditional psychodynamic background, there will be concern that important therapeutic experiences associated with endings are being missed. In psychotherapy, the transferential relationship between the client and the therapist is central to the work. The ending of that relationship is painful and revives intense feelings about separation and individuation, which need attention. The emphasis in family work is more about encouraging family members to use each other as resources, than about reliance on a therapist. 'Since it is the clients who find "the answers" among themselves, the process of disengagement from a therapist and "making it" on their own should be insignificant' (Combrinck-Graham 1980: 508).

In our experience when family work goes well, the closure phase is rarely a period of high anxiety. The periods of highest stress are the referral/induction phase, when a plan of work is being negotiated; and the period approaching the crucial focus, when change is taking place. A fairly common experience is for the family to relax once they are 'over the hump' in the middle phase of the work. If second order change has occurred, the family will have taken a leap to a new integration of the system. They will have made basic changes in their interaction around the problem, and old meanings about relationships and roles will have been replaced by new. They can hardly remember what their earlier anxiety was about, and are friendly but relatively detached in their attitude towards the family workers. 'Families end casually. Family therapists seldom talk about endings. Families usually close the gestalt on their own away from therapy' (Keith and Whitaker 1977).

PROBLEMS ABOUT ENDINGS

Although most families 'end casually', there are some for whom termination does present problems. It is important for us to give attention to the management of these situations, especially as many social workers have difficulty in dealing with closure themselves. The main issues are: panic about separation or independence, and unfinished work.

Workers' anxieties

Workers as well as families fall too easily into the trap of prolonging the agony of parting rather than facing the feelings involved: social workers have real difficulty dealing with endings. Studies of closure in social work agencies indicate that social workers frequently keep cases open longer than necessary. The reasons are partly administrative: it is difficult to set aside time to do a closure summary, or to return to court to ask for an order to be rescinded; but the emotional reactions are also powerful, and seem to be related to a sense of guilt and inadequacy. Bywaters (1975a, 1975b) found that social workers viewed the closure of cases as mainly painful and difficult. The goals of their casework were unlimited; one worker was quoted as saying (typically) 'In a number of cases I could see more than I could have done'. As a result, the social workers regarded the decision to close a case as expedient, because of lack of time or resources, rather than as a positive outcome of the work. In our experience family workers also remain anxious at the end of the contract about whether they have 'done enough'. Training is required to give workers a positive attitude to closure and to help them prepare families for the end of the work.

Family anxieties

Some family members may have had difficult experiences of separation or loss, and ending can revive disabling emotions associated with these painful events in the past. Anxiety rises as the closure date approaches, and the family may fall back on old ways of coping. For example, they may bring an urgent new problem to the last session, and present themselves as helpless and incompetent. The workers should be clear that this is a panic reaction related to the closure, otherwise they will be tempted to continue to prop up the family. They need to acknowledge the power of these feelings, which make adults feel like anxious, abandoned children, and involve family members in sharing their anxieties and feelings of distress and anger. The aim is to draw on the strengths in the family to counter the feelings of panic. One worker might say to the wife 'This is our last meeting, and you are feeling worried. Talk with your husband about how you are both going to tackle this problem'; or to the husband, 'Your wife is feeling anxious, as she did last year after her mother's death. Perhaps you can tell us how the family helped out at that time?' The expression of negative feelings about the work or the workers should be accepted calmly, as part of the mixed feelings which need to be shared as the family moves on.

A real dilemma

Sometimes, in spite of all efforts, at the end of the contract important goals have not been achieved. If the family is highly motivated to continue, a further contract for a limited number of sessions may be negotiated. However, the family worker should consider carefully why the work has not been completed: was a misjudgement made about the pace at which the family could achieve a change? or are family members anxious about their capacity to manage without support? It is important in an extended period of work to stress the family's capacity for independence. This can be done by openly discussing fears about the future, by stressing competence, and by spacing out sessions. When there have been hang-ups in the work, both family and workers may be left with a sense of dissatisfaction, concern about unfinished business, and ambivalence about continuing. (This situation may arise when there has been too little preparation at the referral or induction stage, and no clear agreement reached about the content of the work.) The last two sessions must include a searching review of what has or has not been achieved and why. The decision may be that the family will continue to work on its problems alone; in this case, the final session can be used to help the family think ahead about how problems will be managed. A decision to continue family work should only be made if the air has been cleared, and both sides are committed to continue: then a well-defined but limited contract should be agreed. On no account should the work be allowed to drift.

☐☐ (d₃) A case example related to ending

In the following case example the family workers were convinced of the need to help the Orr family towards independence, but did not attend sufficiently to the family's anxiety as the work reached its closing stages.

Mr and Mrs Orr had a long history of contact with social workers and doctors. All members of the family suffered from various forms of illness, dating back to the birth of the first child, who was diagnosed at birth as being unlikely to survive infancy. Uncertain of their ability to cope with this child, and unable to face their grief, the couple passed their son to the grandparents. At the time of the current referral to social services, this son was 20, still living with his grandparents, handicapped but managing to live a full life; another child with the same heart defect brought up by the parents had recently died. Their only daughter, Betty, was causing problems with which the parents requested help. The social worker who started work with the family responded to the couple's anxiety by trying to meet their endless requests for assistance, without success. At a family workshop consultation it was decided that a male worker should join her and the following hypothesis was made: that in asking for help at this time, the couple was looking for substitute grandparents (the family workers) to avoid another death or disaster in the family. The workers felt that their primary goal should be to acknowledge the couple's lack of confidence and encourage them to accept back their parenting function. As part of their plan only a short contract was negotiated with the family. Although glad of the confidence placed in them and responding well to the help offered, the parents panicked and in the last session again complained at length about Betty's misbehaviour. Not knowing what else to do, the parents had locked her in her room, and only went in to see her when she was beside herself with fury. The workers discussed this with the family in the session, but unfortunately failed to make a link with the parents' own underlying fear and rage and the question: 'To what lengths do *we* have to go, before *we* can obtain help if we need it?' Although concerned, and anxious about how this couple would cope, the workers felt on balance that the plan for closure should go ahead. They arranged a review in three months time. The following week, Mrs Orr took Betty to the hospital after having beaten her; the full Non-Accidental Injury procedure was put into motion and a case conference was held.

The family workers acknowledged that they had not dealt adequately with the family's fear of independence, but remained convinced that they should be given a vote of confidence in their ability to parent successfully. The case conference decision was not to place Betty's name on the At Risk register. The workers saw the parents once more and talked with them about their panic and anger at the time of closure. The parents confirmed that they wanted to cope on their own and believed that they could do so if they were able to call on the social workers in a future crisis. This promise was made, the review held after three months, and no further contact was needed by the family.

MANAGEMENT OF CLOSURE WHEN STATUTORY DUTIES ARE INVOLVED

The timing of closure is not always in a social worker's hands. If the court has made a 2-year Supervision Order on a child, the order may not expire until eighteen months after family work is complete. If a child is on the At Risk register, the social worker is not at liberty to remove the name without the agreement of the case conference. In pursuance of such statutory duties, social workers have in the past continued to visit families long after useful work has been concluded. This is degrading for the family and time-wasting for the social worker. A variety of measures can be put into practice to avoid this happening; examples are given below.

Supervision Orders

1 Ask the court for a Deferred Sentence for a period of six months during which family work can be undertaken.
2 Discussions about family work at a private meeting with magistrates may encourage the magistrates to make shorter supervision orders (six months or one year, instead of two years).
3 The social worker can request the court to make a 6-month supervision order on a child explaining the reasons for the time mentioned in the court report, (for example, a twelve session contract with the family).
4 If work has been successfully completed before the expiry of the order, the worker can return to court and request that the order be rescinded.
5 After family work is finished, the cases of children on supervision orders may be placed 'on review', for visits at 3–6 monthly intervals until the order is complete.
6 If family work is complete, but further work is to be done with the child, the case may be transferred to another worker (for example, a groupworker at the Intermediate Treatment Centre).

Care Orders

If, with the support of a family worker a child subject to a Care Order has been successfully placed at home for six months, the social worker should normally ask the court to rescind the order. Parents should not be expected to care for their own child for any length of time without having their full legal rights.

Children on the At Risk register

1 If the social worker judges that the child is no longer at risk, a case conference should be called to discuss removing the child's name from the register, following which the case can be closed.
2 If the social worker feels that an improvement has been made in the family situation during a period of family work, but is not fully confident that the

situation will not deteriorate, she may agree with the family to a temporary closure of the case, with a review date after a limited time (e.g. three months); and an agreement to be available for help immediately on request from the family or any other concerned person. (If the child is at a day nursery or school, the situation can be monitored carefully with occasional reports to the social worker; this arrangement must be discussed and agreed with the family.)

3 In the case of chronically mis-managing families, who have a history of child abuse, it is still preferable to work with the family in 'bursts' of 6–8 sessions, rather than being in constant weekly attendance over a period of years. Usually it is possible in reading a 'fat file' to observe a pattern or cycle in the recurrence of problems. In the case of the Simpson family, for example, problems recurred every six months: the family workers agreed to visit immediately they were alerted to a difficulty; they would then conduct a number of sessions with the family, and when the work was completed bow out for another few months. The number of sessions varied over the years, sometimes six or eight, sometimes one or two were required. The family felt reassured by this manner of help and compared it favourably to the caring attention of a much loved social worker who had visited weekly for four years. The father in particular said that he had felt his energy drained during that earlier period, and had ceased to take adult initiatives.

The message implicit in all these arrangements is that the family has energy and strengths which can be applied to their own problems and that once a period of family work has been completed the social worker should effectively withdraw.

GUIDELINES FOR CLOSURE

We shall end this chapter by summarizing the discussion in the form of suggestions related to the management of closure. These simple guidelines, some of which have been mentioned already, help to end the work constructively. They should be included in any training programme about family work.

1 If possible prepare the family from the start so that they know when the ending is likely to be.
2 Discuss the ending in time to allow family members to do their 'worry work'. Be sensitive to expressions of panic by the family, in words or behaviour, at the thought of being without the support of the workers. Allow for expressions of negative feelings, and respond to them fully without backing off from closure.
3 Review the progress of the family in dealing with problems about which they have been concerned. Rehearse how the family will manage new problems when they arise.
4 Talk about the strengths and achievements of each family member.
5 Play down – but do not deny – the worker's contribution in the progress achieved.
6 Reassure the family that they can contact the agency/workers again if they need

help at some future date. Talk about the strengths in asking for help at the right time.

7 If the atmosphere is right, spend some time enjoying the family. (Often photograph albums are brought out at the last session to share past events with the workers.)

8 Say goodbye thoughtfully and without hurry, speaking to each person individually.

□□ **(e) Activities for further learning**

Using the network

1 Create a 'network map' (see *Figure 3*) for one family with whom you have worked – try to guess what influences each of its sub-systems might have had on that family.

2 Assume you are the worker for the Bailey family and are preparing yourself for attending the case conference with the CGU about Mary:

    (a) Ask your training/supervision group to role play the Bailey family and discuss with them what information you may share at the case conference.

    (b) What part(s) of the work with the Baileys would you have considered essential for sharing in the case conference?

    (c) Now ask your training/supervision group to enact the case conference and role play the worker. Then ask for feedback about the terms you have used (behaviour descriptions or attribution of feelings) and whether you have conveyed too much or too little.

Maintenance strategies

1 Recall the family in which you grew up – describe them to a friend or a colleague and decide whether they were 'slow movers' or 'fast movers'.

2 Invent a 'slow moving' family, with whom you have just finished an intensive family work programme. You are responsible for a child in the family, who is under a 2-year supervision order, with eighteen months still to run.

    (a) Decide how frequently you will offer follow-up sessions.

    (b) Prepare a case for presentation to your supervisor about your plans for this family, especially in view of the supervision order.

    (c) With the help of a colleague, role play your planned discussion with your supervisor.

Continued on next page

Continued from previous page

Ending

1 Recall a significant 'ending' in your own life. Write down what your feelings were at the time. What helped you to move on?
2 Imagine a family which feels panic at the prospect of closure. In your training group, role play this family. Practise ways of helping them to face the future without the support of a social worker.

PART III
FURTHER ISSUES

The story of working with the Baileys has ended, but some further issues remain that are important in family work.

Part III consists of three concluding chapters. Having expanded on cases that had apparently gone well in the previous chapters, we now pause to consider the other side – cases that appear to fail.

In Chapter 12 we examine 'when a failure is a failure' and think what may prevent work from going wrong. In Chapter 13 we discuss various training and supervisory goals in family work and how to set up the organizational arrangements to provide them within a Social Services Department.

The final chapter (Chapter 14) explores the wider implications of our discussion. There are certain skills that may be applied to social work tasks other than family work, and furthermore, we believe that system theory, upon which family work is based, has much to offer elsewhere. We demonstrate one of the potential applications in an example from adoption and fostering.

The book ends with the suggestion that planning an intervention systemically may entail asking four questions about: the type of feedback used, the system approached, the level of intervention, and the timing of delivering it.

12 / FACING FAILURE

Much can be learned from looking at those cases where we think that we have failed. Sharing our failures can be healing and in many cases amusing. From previous chapters it might have seemed that the practitioners concerned had been a group of very competent family workers who rarely make mistakes. At this point it is important to remind everyone of the reality of social work within the local authority setting. The doubts and worries which come to all practising social workers while dealing with the misery, pain, and suffering of clients who come to social services, often as a last resort, are also an integral part of working with families in the way advocated in this book. So much written by family therapists seems to be about charismatic personalities who are able to think on their feet without any problem and who seemingly perform magic. Without denigrating the very real achievements of some of the experts it is important to be able to see that this style of work can be used by an ordinary local authority social worker who is interested in, and committed to attempting to put some of the theory she has learned into practice and to learn from what she is trying to do, whether it is judged a success or failure. The importance of actually working with families while learning about the method cannot be stressed strongly enough. As mentioned in Chapter 13, the support, encouragement, and criticism of other workers in the family workshop setting are essential. Everyone fails with some cases. Reviewing and discussing what happened is the most essential next step.

Recently, more accounts of failures have been published than ever before. Some of these are frameworks for understanding failures in family therapy (Jenkins, Hildrebrand, and Lask 1982; Treacher and Carpenter 1982; Carpenter *et al.* 1982). The purpose of this chapter is not to develop another framework, but simply to give some examples from practice and to draw some conclusions where possible.

WHEN IS FAILURE REALLY A FAILURE?

Are some failures really so? How does one define a failure? We need to be less vague and try to identify events or situations that may at first look like or feel like a failure, but on second thoughts would not be judged as such. For example, in one of the family workshops the workers assessed 27 families with whom they had worked during one year: various levels of change were seen in 14 of them; 'No change or deterioration' in 10; 'Too early to judge' in the remaining 3. The 'no change' category included several cases which had never properly been engaged in the work. In looking closer at each of these categories they began to look far more heterogeneous. Quite a lot depended on what changes were considered by the workers as 'an improvement' and how soon they expected the improvement to be evident.

When is failure really a failure?

Here are three examples:

Delayed action

It seems that the speed with which families react to a new situation varies considerably (Olson, Sprenkle, and Russel 1979). So, the worker should not be surprised if the family's reactions to her interventions vary too. Some families may shift immediately, while others may take quite a while before any change becomes evident.

The Wood family consisted of mother, teenage daughter, and two younger boys. The family was close-knit and the inexperienced worker felt useless. She wanted to help them become less dependent on each other. Jason, the youngest, was not going to school, and had committed a minor offence. The older children were unable to leave mother who was over-protective. The worker felt sucked into the system, but kept up her visits to the family and on the advice of her supervisor used a paradox; she told the family that she did not think they would ever be able to separate, they would not leave mother, and she did not believe they would ever get jobs, go to school, etc. She did not believe they were likely to change in the near future. She then pulled out of the situation. After a delay of some months, she met Jason in the street. He told her he had left school and had got a job (the place of work was across the road from the social service area office!) and that his sister had moved out of the home. It appeared that the paradox had succeeded.

The family break-up

There is often an unspoken assumption, particularly in social services, that removing a child into care or the separation of parents are always failures. It is high time that this assumption is questioned. It probably rests on the notion of the family as an organic whole that should never break, a cell that should physically hold its parts together. However, the family as an interrelated network of individual human beings cannot cease; it can only change. A structural change such as separation or a departure of one member is in no way the end of the psychological attachments among family members, although it may well introduce changes within them. The confusion about 'the break up' of a family, a transformation through which all families go to some extent, even if some families seem to do it more abruptly than others, is destructive to both social workers and the families they try to help. We cannot assume that separations are always for the worst. For example, the Brown family, was really two families − a re-constituted family. The three older children were siblings from the father's first marriage. Their mother had died very tragically; they never recovered from this and wanted no part of the new family, a cohabitee and three much younger children. For a long time many agencies, including the local authority Social Services Department had been putting a tremendous effort into helping this 'family' to get together and become a 'new' family and not to eject the two eldest children. They were referred to the family workshop with a clear message, 'Don't let this family eject these two children'. When the workshop members assessed the case it seemed that it was acceptable for the eldest, aged 19, to leave the family and that the girl aged 16 had found some relatives to stay with who were happy to have her. It seemed in fact that it was a fairly reasonable way for the family to have decided to deal with the problem. A brief contact to affirm this with the family sufficed. In fact there was much less tension and the parents were able to manage the rest of the family once the two older children had gone.

Being at a loss

Some practitioners feel that whenever they are confused and unable to find out what to do they must be failing. This happens frequently in working with families and needs to be questioned closely. There may be brief stages in family work when the worker's confusion is in fact the best sign that a certain type of change is taking place. This is not to say that all confusion is necessarily creative, but to stress that as users of system theory we have come to accept that one type of change involves the workers in being at a loss; feeling that they have exhausted all their knowledge and resources and are still getting nowhere. This type of change is called 'second order change'. It is different from other changes, when some part of behaviour is altered (first order change), since it entails a change in the meaning of, and the values associated with, behaviour in the family system. During a time-limited contract second order change often happens in the middle of the series. The workers come out of the session gloomy and confused, even hurt. Nothing they have tried has worked; they have had enough and are willing to admit failure. They have thoughts of referring the family elsewhere or using their statutory powers – anything to introduce some certainty. It is vitally important to understand the paradox of this situation. A second order change is achieved by the family, plus the workers, changing the rules of behaviour together. It is in these moments just when we feel we have totally failed, that we have in fact begun to succeed. When approaching the crucial focus (Chapter 9), nine times out of ten the workers are feeling at a loss. The confusion which is actually the shift to second order change is a time of agony and despair for everyone and if the workers do not get infected by it then they are not 'with it'. The worker has to deal with the confusion and pain within herself without changing her line with the family. Two workers remembered the case of the Trent family where they admitted to each other that, after the fourth session, if either had been on their own they would have given in to the pressure and received the daughter into care. They were absolutely panic-stricken because they walked out of the session having resisted the family's pressure and were very worried about the girl's safety: 'We walked out because we could do nothing. We said we were leaving. We were not going to receive Jenny into care because we believed it was not necessary'. After the workers had had a sleepless night, the family contacted them: they had resolved things constructively and no longer wanted the child in care.

When workers feel hopeless and despairing it is so hard for them to remember that this can be part of the process of change. It is important for a supervisor or workshop colleagues to be able to stand outside the therapeutic system to some extent at this point and reassure the workers that this 'mess' is constructive.

THE TRUE FAILURE

Having said all this, we should also recognize that mistakes and misjudgements do occur and should be noted before it is too late for help. They can probably be judged only over time when a pattern begins to emerge that, for all we know, does indicate some form of failure. Very rarely, if ever, can we identify a failure on the basis of what happened during one session. However, when events begin over time to fall into a pattern, they may add up to an indication of failure. Here are some of the patterns which caused concern in family workshops in which the authors have been involved:

The family is not working on the problems

This is obviously a sign that the family is not engaged by the workers. Sessions are often cancelled, important family members are missing, and yet there is no sign that the problem for which the family came to the agency is resolved.

A lot has happened but nothing has changed

Although family members may attend the sessions and fully participate in them there is no visible shift in any of their behaviour, nor any alleviation of the presenting problem. Since there is usually a hidden pay-off to the presenting problem (a delinquent teenager takes attention away from severe marital difficulties) it can be gratifying to the family to discuss it, and even illuminating. However, if neither the process of communication, nor the structural arrangements in the family shift as a result and the presenting problem persists, the workers may have to accept this as a failure. Sometimes the workers report to supervisors or colleagues that they are bored by the family in these circumstances – the boredom gives a clue to what is happening in the system.

The Yo-Yo game

It may be possible to deal with the presenting problem as it is manifested in relation to one member, but after a while another 'problem' appears in relation to a different family member, usually of a similar type. For example, the workers may congratulate each other on preventing the reception into care of one child, and three months later are asked to take another child into care. This may indicate that the family system has not changed in spite of a temporary relief earlier on.

The systemic mess

This type of difficulty occurs when the family system is particularly complex, secretive, or confusing. It is difficult to see the wood for the trees and interventions are misdirected. Sometimes the worker is aware that she does not know what the system is, yet she tries to intervene anyway. In one family workshop the co-workers took a referral where the children's disturbance was very worrying. They knew that the problem in the family was that the marriage was a secret marriage: the parents had officially separated but the father was secretly living in the home. Although the workers knew he was there and tried to engage him, he would not join the family sessions that they set up. They spent much time and trouble trying to work with the mother and trying to hook the father in through her, knowing that this was the crucial issue. It was not successful. It may be that they tried too hard, but the family was not able to join in any of the family work.

The workers' failure

Although the four sets of circumstances described above are indications of impending failure, supervisors and colleagues can be helpful in pointing out what is going on and helping the workers either to change their interventions or to decide that the family is not open to family work at this stage. If the latter is true, as might be the case in the first set, attempts can be made to keep things on ice or withdraw for a time, as discussed in Chapter 11.

It would be helpful if it could be said that a certain worker's behaviour produces a failure, but one has to be very wary of doing this. Therefore, although it cannot be shown which mistakes lead to which failures, some suggestions can be made as to how some difficulties have been associated with the consequent failures.

The worker's lack of skill and/or knowledge. Even with the best training in the world, the actual delivery of the best chosen intervention can go awry. It is one thing to understand which intervention might help best in a given situation and even to role-play it in a workshop session. It is quite another matter to deliver it to the family appropriately.

The workers are at a loss and don't know it. Supervisors and colleagues need to be alert for the times when workers' interventions are inappropriate or ineffective. They may be repeating the same intervention and not producing a shift in the family behaviour; they may be unclear why they are doing something and cannot talk about it. Inexperienced family workers take time to develop the skills which help families to change.

Failure to negotiate with other agencies. As mentioned in Chapter 9, often when the crucial focus is reached the family turn to other professionals in order to avoid the change that the family workers are trying to achieve with them. This is very common and is guaranteed to happen to every family worker at some time. It is so easy to assume that the 'sensible doctor' would not decide to make such a recommendation, or that granny did not exert such a considerable influence.

The supervisory confusion. A difficulty may appear in a co-working or supervisory sub-system. When people co-work they need to invest effort in straightening out the relationship between them if their work with the family is to have one direction at any particular time. One worker recalled an occasion when she asked her co-worker to leave the room with her so that they could discuss what they could offer the family. The co-worker said 'No, I don't work that way'. This threw them both into confusion.

A situation where a supervisory relationship is not clarified can be fraught with difficulties. The supervisor also needs to see that she is sufficiently detached so as not to be caught up in the family system herself. A worker remembered her first case when she and her co-worker became completely enmeshed in the family system, picking up the family dynamic and reflecting the rebellious adolescent and passively angry mother within their own relationship. Their supervisor was helpless to get them out of the mess and one aspect which contributed to her helplessness was that in the other work of the Area the supervisor and supervisee positions were reversed. The reversal of roles had not been worked on. Assumptions had been made that were emotionally problematic.

Lack of experience in using supervisory tools can lead to amazing situations too, as happened when one workshop first started to use video equipment. Because of the workers' apprehension at their first video session they had forgotten to tell the clients of the supervisors' presence or to set up an arrangement to enable the supervisors to call them out if they thought they were stuck. The supervisory group remained helpless to intervene as the workers became more and more confused.

Further issues

There are some ground rules that apply to delivery of all interventions. These are called 'core conditions', which tell us how to communicate with our clients and should be adopted (Egan 1975), but it seems that two of the most common areas of failure are in dealing with anger and sexuality.

Anger. Too many workers seem to feel that expressing anger is unacceptable. They are often able to acknowledge the angry feelings in a client and even to reflect them back, but rarely to directly express anger themselves. A worker remembered an occasion when she was dealing with a family very like the first example in this chapter, and she told the mother to shut up, saying what 'a rotten job' she was doing and that she could do better than that. The mother then told all her friends – 'That's the place to go. They shout at you, but you feel great afterwards'. One can speculate on whether or not the people drawn to social work find it hard to show anger towards those they try to help. The culture from which most British social workers come must also contribute to the feeling of some that it is wrong or impolite to show anger.

Sexuality. Although we know that it is sometimes very important to talk about sex freely and openly, many of us are paralysed when it comes to enabling clients to discuss their feelings in this area. This could be connected with the image of local authority workers being more concerned with child management and practicalities, or it could come from our own personal inhibitions. One worker found it hard to broach the matter of a mother's strong lesbian preferences which he felt to be at the root of the family's difficulties. Until he was able to make some acknowledgement of this, his interventions were useless. Although this worker was very experienced he found it extremely difficult to allow these feelings to come into the open, but he was aware that by not doing this he was colluding with the family. Sometimes it is possible to use analogies in this area when it is judged too disturbing for the family to be direct. What does seem to be certain is that if the workers collude through embarrassment or uncertainty with a family secret then they have become sucked into this family's system and are then powerless to help.

It is hoped that the reader has now some idea about the sort of failures most family workers in local authority social services departments experience. It is by no means an exhaustive exploration of failure and no doubt many people will have their own special experiences to add. Before ending this chapter it is important to bring together some of the lessons that can be learned from looking at our failures. It would be marvellous if a recipe for preventing failure could be given, but of course there is not one. The best that the authors feel they can offer is a series of questions that can be kept in the workers' minds so that the possibilities of failure can be detected early enough, hopefully to correct them or to prevent them turning into final failures.

Before work
  (a) Are the co-workers compatible? Have they spent enough time with one another?
  (b) Is the worker aware of her own feelings and how they could affect the family work?
  (c) Has it been made clear to the family what is being offered?
  (d) Has the work been negotiated with the family and other agencies? Have other people in the family network been considered?

During work
  (a) Is the time right for the family to engage in change?
  (b) Has the whole family been engaged?
  (c) Have the other interested agencies been kept in touch with what the workers are doing?
  (d) Are the workers able to explain what they are attempting and why?
  (e) Is this intervention really failing, or have the workers reached the crucial focus with its accompanying confusion engendered by the need for second order change?
  (f) Is the supervisory sub-system communicating clearly and sufficiently detached?
  (g) Is it really failure for the family, or have they dealt with the problem in a way the worker has not anticipated?

After work
  (a) What did the worker do and what did she not do?
  (b) Has the presenting problem been dealt with?
  (c) What could have been done differently?
  (d) Were the worker's expectations realistic?

13 / TRAINING, SUPERVISION, AND HOW TO ORGANIZE FOR THEM

Upon completion of training social workers will have been introduced to a variety of complex theoretical concepts but may not have sufficient practical experience to support these. Fortunately, employers are increasingly aware of the need to create opportunities which allow for integration of theory and practice through in-service training, and supervisors in particular can be instrumental in helping workers make these links so that their intervention is appropriate and skilled. In this chapter we discuss basic issues concerning in-service training and supervision and then describe some outlines for organizing these in a local authority office.

TRAINING AND SUPERVISION

The challenge of training for family work is not only a problem for newly qualified workers for it often takes a few years of practice before the social worker is ready to experiment with different methods of intervention; after the initial consolidation of basic training she is ready for another layer of additional learning and refinement of techniques. The timing of this varies, of course, from individual to individual, but interest in learning family work skills usually follows from the worker's awareness that one-person interviewing techniques do not always work within multi-person interviews. Something different is required and the worker begins to realize that additional theory and skills are needed to enrich her style and method of intervention.

A worker coming to this recognition can be heard to report 'I finally saw Mr and Mrs Brown together!' (said with a sense of achievement), but this is often followed by a more tempered voice, 'It was like being a referee in a boxing match' or, 'It was like having an observer in on my conversation with one or the other'. Another often heard complaint is 'I saw Mr and Mrs Brown together with their three children . . . we couldn't talk for more than a few minutes without one or other of the children interrupting'. If the worker and supervisor are not prepared to think about family work methods in these situations the worker may continue struggling or may give it up as a 'bad job' and return to excluding Mr Brown and the three children prematurely.

Making the transition from one to multi-person interviewing is one of the first leaps required for family work. Equipped with system theory (see Chapter 2) the worker is now ready to begin experimentation. Chapter 3 is aimed at giving the reader some ideas of how to prepare oneself and the support one needs from colleagues.

Recording

One of the crucial steps is to re-examine the process of recording. Even if video equipment and tape recorders are used there is still the problem of finding a brief way of summerizing and organizing the material on paper. Recording of sessions is often a much avoided subject – workers hate doing it, supervisors hate requesting it! We cannot attempt to address here each worker's special difficulties in 'getting it down on paper', but there are ways to help organize the worker's thoughts in order to record important aspects of the session and help plan for the next.

The following are main headings suggested for consideration:

(a) The major theme – it is important to be brief and succinct.
(b) The worker's reaction to the session – the immediate feelings, again one or two words can express this.
(c) The entrance – how were you met and received, by whom, who was there, how did the session begin?
(d) Worker's behaviour/family's behaviour – here you record verbal and observed behaviour sequences between you and the family as they followed each other during the session.
(e) Exit – how did you leave, how did the session end?
(f) Unfinished business – a listing will do.
(g) Comments and observations.
(h) Plan for the next session.

In-service training

Let us turn now to in-service training. Training for family work has become an apprenticed type of programme in which colleagues may help one another hypothesize about the problem to be tackled and practise interventions aimed at promoting change. A. C. R. Skynner addresses this point and states:

'We have come to realize that growth takes place through challenge and response, through the intrusion into a system of information from its surroundings which disturbs its stability, demands the development of new capacities and coping skills, and so alters its repertoire of programs in a more flexible and adoptable direction. But this change in fundamental principle must affect the therapist and therapeutic team and the helping profession generally as much as those they seek to help. If the family can change only through an increased permeability of its boundaries and the entry of new values and concepts from the wider world carried by the therapist, so personal and professional growth in the therapists themselves can continue only insofar as they are open to constant criticism and correction by their colleagues.'

(Skynner 1976: 274)

Individual supervision therefore must give way to include other methods and structures. Thus, we have seen that co-therapy, the use of video, one-way screens, or tape recorders have led on to the development of supervisors sitting in on sessions and interventions coming from a supervisory team. (For further discussion of these supervisory techniques see Whiffen and Byng-Hall 1982.)

There is currently a debate amongst family workers about the best way to train for family work and help workers develop their expertise in enabling families to change. Jay Hayley states that 'A therapist can only learn about (therapy) by doing it. All other training activity is peripheral, if not irrelevant. Ideally he learns to do therapy by doing it guided by a supervisor at the moment the therapy is happening' (Haley 1976: 181). This model stresses the need for workers to learn the techniques without necessarily needing to focus on personal growth of the worker. Minuchin states that 'Although different therapists might agree on a therapeutic goal for a particular family, their technique for achieving that goal will vary. Therapists having individual personalities and skills, develop idiosyncratic ways of relating. They can use themselves better if they learn to know and accept their own styles' (Minuchin 1974: 256). Lidz carries the point further by suggesting that 'The inexperienced therapist can inadvertantly promote disorganization of an individual or a family because of his countertransference to a family member, his transference of his own family problems into the situation, his exasperation with the rigidity or lack of empathy of family members, his shock at the cruelties that may go on within a family, his narcissistic needs or simply by lack of recognition of his own limitations' (Lidz 1974: xv). It seems to us that these stances do not necessarily contradict one another and indeed, polarization between the insight orientated approaches and more behavioural approaches places workers in some danger of not benefitting from the perspectives that each provide. Social workers are trained differently and also are faced with numerous tasks and different family structures. Because of this, we need to be able to draw on the various approaches and to utilize them as appropriately as we can.

DIMENSIONS OF TRAINING AND SUPERVISION

Without overstating the case we must recognize that learning to work with families involves dealing with people in distress and this affects our own most profound emotions and inevitably causes discomfort. Emergent with these feelings are all the individual and complex ways of dealing with them. It follows that the individual worker must be helped at least to anticipate and recognize her own reactions if she is going to be free to see clearly what the family needs. For instance, a worker whose own family life influenced her to expect that raised voices immediately preceded someone getting hurt, will need to know this if she is to be free to tolerate raised voices in her client families and still understand what it means for *them*.

The more we know our own reactions to being the odd one out – being yelled at by an angry mother, having an elder brother tell on us – and the freer we are in recognizing our own values and assumptions, the better we shall be at discerning what these mean for the client family and what level of change is needed in their system. We can work on our hunches only after we have done our own work of sorting out and knowing our own reactions to stress.

Supervision within groups, sculpting families, or role-playing aspects of sessions can all help the individual worker unstick herself in order to progress on the road of helping families change. For instance, a worker who is getting stuck while talking about a case or who is not really allowing the group to help her think about the work could be asked to sculpt the family instead of giving more verbal information. This involves the other group members immediately and cuts across the verbal flooding. A worker who feels a family is succeeding in disabling her could be asked to role-play a sequence of the next session so that she can project herself forward and exercise her 'muscles' by looking more closely at the delivery of her interventions. A worker who feels stuck in her work could be asked to role-play the family member identified by her as the most 'difficult', so that she can be 'difficult' herself, understand the need behind the behaviour and then free herself to look at other ways of intervening. Alongside these individual examples will be the group's interaction and their involvement in reflecting what occurs within the family sessions due to their identification with the client family (Mattison 1977). The discussion and behaviour of the group (in their attempts to work with the family's problems) may reflect aspects of the family dynamics and this will need to be clarified and resolved if the group is to continue to help the worker. Examples of this phenomenon take many forms. One worker brought a case stating she did not know which way to proceed in the work; she described the family and the way the work was developing. Group members were asking questions of the worker but were doing so in a delicate and somewhat conciliatory manner. This was noticed and examined as related to the family's own behaviour. It emerged that the worker feared pressing the mother just as family members over protected her. Through identification of this, the worker was then helped to practise ways of rephrasing the issues needing to be raised and to anticipate the mother's possible reactions. Equally the group was helped to become more direct in their attempts to engage the worker over these aspects of the work.

Furthermore, beyond the reflection process there is the dynamic that evolves in the training/supervisory group as such. Like any other group the training/supervisory one will have to resolve certain dynamic issues; contracting should be clear, power and its different sources worked out, closeness should be allowed yet contained as appropriate to the task, and individual differentiation among members encouraged. Quite a lot depends on the working style of the group leader. If the group is led by two trainers/supervisors the relationship between them will also determine the resolution of these issues. Within a healthy and open system specific skills can be rehearsed, achievements promptly reinforced through praise, and workers' skills explicitly and consistently monitored.

Finally, 'live supervision' either through the use of one-way mirrors, 'ear bugs', or having a supervisor in the room go further still to help the worker shape her interventions in more concrete and accurate ways. Each requires the worker to be willing to expose her style to her colleagues and to be open to use their advice and contributions. This may be difficult at first but it becomes easier as trust is established and you begin to see the advantages for your and your colleagues' work.

We have made only brief and general comments here about styles of training and supervision, which obviously require much more space than this handbook allows (see Whiffen and Byng-Hall 1982).

The culture of local authority social services offices in Britain deserves special attention if social workers in them are to apply family therapy skills effectively. The by now well-known family workshop groups are planted within organizations that have their own mandates and understandings. We can see that both growth (Iveson, Sharps, and Whiffen 1971) and skill (Adams 1980) oriented workshops have been adopted. In the second half of this chapter we share our own organizational experience of forming and leading both types in a local authority office.

ORGANIZING FOR TRAINING AND SUPERVISION

It will be good to see the day when every team leader in a local authority office has the knowledge and experience to provide guidance in family work. At present this situation is some while away. The shortage of knowledge in this area among senior social workers may seem an insurmountable block to progress in family work. However, it is a block only as long as we stay within the traditional hierarchical model of management, where the supervisory input has to come exclusively from the team leader to the team member. There is by now enough experience to suggest that the classically hierarchical model is only one option. An alternative model is called the 'Dual Influence' model (Rowbottom, Hey, and Billis 1974).

The dual influence model

This model recognizes that few of us possess specialized knowledge about *all* social work activities. It also assumes that workers are willing to share power and are able to communicate between themselves about their differing areas of knowledge.

If these assumptions hold, it is useful to differentiate the guidance input that workers need into two types:

Method input: this input concerns expertise in a method of work and includes, for example, specific moves that the worker will make during the session with a family. For instance, the worker may be advised to offer the family a specific growth game and shown how to do that.

Operational input: this input concerns the activities of the worker in relation to the organizational and legal requirements that bind her as an employee of an agency. For example, how to handle confidentiality in cases of risk to life or limb; how to negotiate with the court about an Interim Care Order; a particularly brief supervision order; or convince the EWO to delay court proceedings until a certain phase of family work is over.

It is obvious that in a large organization the operational input has to be in the hands of a person accountable for the work, usually the team leader or another member of the management group. More leeway exists with regard to the method inputs. Some area offices have been known to invite an outside 'expert' for this purpose. The advantage of an outsider is that workers have respect for an established 'expert' and are usually prepared to take advice from her. The disadvantages of an outsider are that she may inadvertantly foster the local worker's belief in the existence of a mighty body of knowledge which is above the head of the run-of-the-mill social worker: she is also unfamiliar with local procedures. This makes it more difficult for the worker to relate the operational input (from the team leader) to the method input (from the outsider). The outsider is also only available for the sessions arranged and will, therefore, not be able to offer a method input at a time of unpredicted crisis.

For these reasons, we have tended whenever possible, to favour a worker in the same agency as the source of method input. However, there is more than one way of locally organizing this input.

Applications of the dual influence model

Ideally, the organization created should fit the sort of method your workers choose. As mentioned in the previous section, training in family work has been offered in different ways. The training styles seem to be ranged between those which emphasize active development of 'the use of self' to those stressing 'skill training'. There is, of course, a great deal of overlap between the two, but the accent on 'the use of self' will lead to one structure for a family workshop , while the accent on 'skill training' will lead to another. We do not know that one is better than the other, but it seems important to identify the sort of method input offered and then organize the family workshop to match. Although in reality few adopt purely one or the other, experience suggests that when the method input is slanted towards 'the use of self' a 'consultancy' model is adequate. However, when this input has an accent on 'skill training' it is necessary to move into the supervisory model. Let us see what is involved in developing each.

Accent on the use of self and the consultancy model

In this model the method input will focus on the understanding of the interaction between the underlying feelings and fantasies of family members and those of the worker, and how these relate to what actually takes place in the session.

The person who offers the workers the method input is mainly concerned with mechanisms such as projection, identification, displacement, and denial. She helps to elucidate these in the family as well as in the ways the workers react to the family. She is less active with regard to coaching the workers. It is the emotional import they bring to bear on what they do that concerns her most. Although in the process of consultation she may raise suggestions for some specific moves, her main concern is that whatever the workers choose to do, they are free of the distraction created by the above mechanisms. Her intervention is aimed more at clarification than coaching the workers behaviourally. Therefore, this model provides relatively more freedom for each worker to develop her own style. As she does this it is left to her to negotiate changes in the operational input with her respective team leader. It is the *way* she uses them that is different. In such cases the method input is less likely to clash with the accepted operational input. The latter may remain closer to that offered for other social work activities. Statutory powers may be used in much the same way and relatively fewer new demands will be made on other agencies such as schools or hospitals. Because the operational input can be negotiated individually it seems possible to leave accountability in the hands of the team leader responsible for the work load of each family worker. This will mean that the family workshop group can be comprised of workers from a number of teams. They all receive their method input from the same consultant who will make suggestions concerning the operational input, but will have to have these ratified by the worker's team leader. This is the consultancy model. The family workshop group has the power to make only suggestions which ultimately need to be ratified by the respective team leaders. This arrangement can work. The advantage is that it fits into the existing managerial structure and encourages sharing of the specialist knowledge with other team leaders when suggestions come back to them for approval. Schematically it will look like this:

Figure 5 Minimal structure for a consultancy family workshop

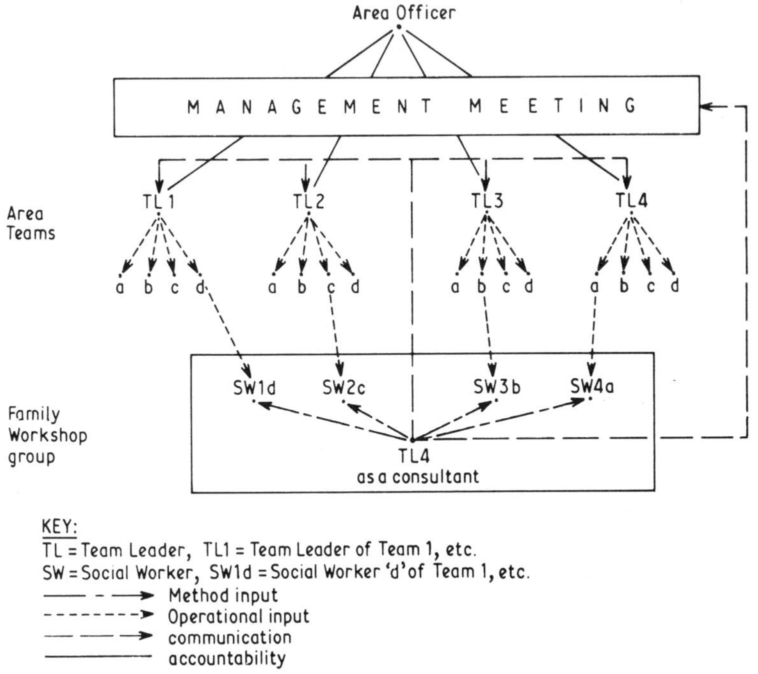

KEY:
TL = Team Leader, TL1 = Team Leader of Team 1, etc.
SW = Social Worker, SW1d = Social Worker 'd' of Team 1, etc.
——— – ——→ Method input
- - - - - - -→ Operational input
—— —— —→ communication
—————— accountability

Having said that the consultancy model *can* work does not imply that it always will. It should be stressed that the consultancy model has an Achilles' heel built into it. Not only does it allow workers to bypass and undermine their team leaders' authority; the model makes the family workshop group vulnerable to projections and displacements from the rest of the area office. This is so because in the consultancy model feelings are given such prominence that the group may be perceived by those outside it as a 'therapy group'. If the rest of the area office does not share intimate feelings openly the family workshop group can become the kitchen for preparatory work on unresolved feelings. If the rest of the area office struggles with hidden agendas of undisclosed feelings those who open up (in our case the family workshop group members) may be used in the same way that a single family member is used when he/she dares speak his/her mind – he/she is labelled eccentric, neurotic, indulgent, etc.

It is important to develop an effective communication culture in the area office as a whole. However, until this is achieved it is wise to build safeguards for the family workshop group. Two of these come immediately to mind.

(a) The family workshop consultant should be one of the team leaders. The fact that the consultant is also a team leader enables her to anticipate the operational input offered by other team leaders under this model, and help the workers reconcile it with her own. Her position allows her direct and informal access to each of the team leaders which she can use when required.

(b) The family workshop should be discussed in the management meeting. In order to prevent all sorts of fantasies, feelings of envy, displacements of frustration etc. from building up around the family workshop group and thus undermining its work, the team leader who acts as the consultant (TL4 in *Figure 5*) should take the initiative and ask the management group to review the development of the family workshop group periodically. This will give the consultant an opportunity not only to find out what fantasies are building up in other team leaders' minds, but also to give them direct feedback that will prevent fantasies in the first place. Questions about operational directives can be clarified during these reviews.

Accent on skill training and the supervisory model

The method input may also focus on the actual strategies that the family workers employ during the session. The person who offers such an input adopts a more behavioural slant and works out specific steps that the workers will take with the family. This may include coaching them in the use of sculpting, designing a behaviour change programme, rehearsing how to reframe behaviour etc. Under this model the accent is on skill first. The underlying feelings are taken up only as and when they can be seen to undermine the use of a certain skill. The input is, therefore, more directive than reflective. It includes specific suggestions as to the timing of the use of statutory powers, the wording of certain messages, and the like. It may, therefore, intrude upon the use of the accepted operational input. Indeed, some crucial changes in the accepted operational input may be required (modification of review procedures on Care Orders, special conditions for reception into care, mental health admission, etc.). Because of this intimate relationship between skill training and the operational input, it seems better to contain both of them in the family workshop group. The supervisory model takes care of this by insisting that work done within the family workshop is wholly supervised by its own leaders.

This does not mean that all the input has to come from one person. The family workshop group can be led by two people. One should have the seniority of team leader or above. This person takes care of all the operational input for the group. The other can be a senior practitioner or a specialist family worker who takes care of the method input. Schematically the supervisory model will look like this:

Figure 6 Minimal structure for a supervisory family workshop

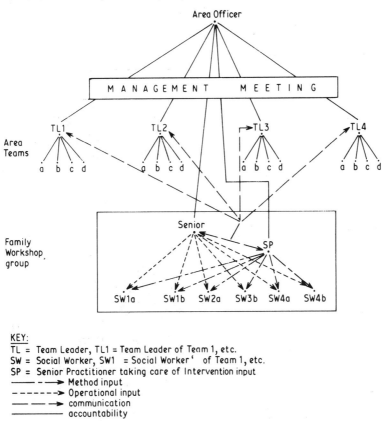

KEY:
TL = Team Leader, TL1 = Team Leader of Team 1, etc.
SW = Social Worker, SW1 = Social Worker' of Team 1, etc.
SP = Senior Practitioner taking care of Intervention input
——— — → Method input
– – – – – – → Operational input
—— — — → communication
——————— accountability

This close 'marriage' of method and operational inputs gives the family workshop considerable freedom to innovate; trying new interventions and modifying existing procedures to match them. However, the model has its own perils too. The 'marriage' can produce an enmeshed 'family'. The family workshop group members can begin to imagine that they are self-sufficient because all their needs seem to be met inside the group. This illusion is to be avoided. If it takes root the group is soon perceived as an elitist venture. Envy and resentment begin to surround it and soon referrals of families thin out or only inappropriate families are referred. Workers undertaking to practise within the supervisory model have, therefore, to re-double their efforts towards keeping their group an open system. The onus is particularly on the two leaders. They have not only to bring the family workshop group for periodical review at the management meeting, but to take every opportunity to communicate to the team leaders the general direction of their members' work. Of course, this cannot happen coherently if the two leaders do not continuously exchange views and feelings between themselves. Not only is this crucial for conveying a meaningful feedback to the other team leaders, but without it the leadership of the family workshop group will run into serious difficulties. While each of the leaders retains responsibility for one of the respective inputs, a certain degree of role overlap is healthy. The senior social worker should feel free to comment on specific interventions and the senior practitioner should be allowed to raise ideas about policy and procedures. This enables a creative cross-fertilization and, furthermore, prevents splitting of the workshop members into those loyal to one against those loyal to the other. It also presents to the members a healthy model of conflict resolution and co-operation. However, the axis between the two leaders needs special care. They need to meet on their own periodically to sort out their roles and the overlap between them, as well as how they both contribute to a healthy group culture. If they can enlist the help of a third uninvolved party (the area officer or a training officer) who gives them neutral feedback, all the better. When later on more family workshop groups are set up, the leaders can form themselves into a steering group. Creating a steering group is very useful indeed, because it helps communication within the whole department and, even more importantly, gives each pair of leaders an opportunity to discuss the leadership of their group with uninvolved yet committed workers who can give the leaders feedback as to how to improve their respective and joint leadership.

Organizing a referral system

The structure of family workshops tends to grow and become more diversified over time. Each new group has its own ideas and innovations which are part of that spark characteristic of a healthy and creative environment. The steering group helps to keep the parts together by devising procedures that accommodate the diversity among the groups. For example, in one area office there was at one time one group for people with relatively little or no experience of family work or family therapy, called the training group. They concentrated on learning time-limited approaches along the focused family work line and visited the families at their homes. More experienced workers joined two other groups. One concentrated on the systemic approach with the extensive use of video facilities. The other was interested particularly in a quick response to families and manned a Thursday afternoon duty slot where families were

Figure 7 A family workshop referral system

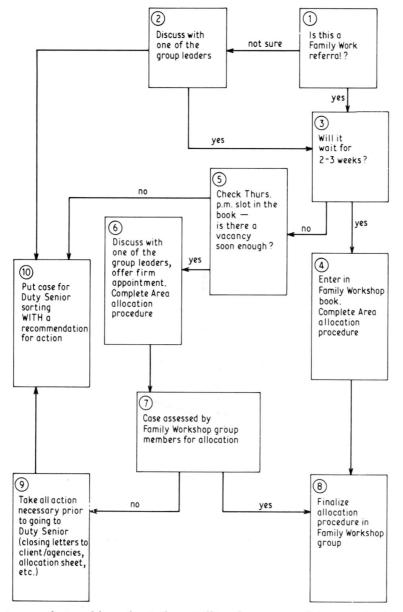

This version was designed for us by Graham Willis, who was one of the group leaders.

seen by a pair of workers on the spot. The steering group saw it as its job to co-ordinate the referrals to all those groups. A referral book was opened in the duty room along with a book for the Thursday afternoon duty slot. All the leaders were prepared to be consulted as and when the need arose. They judged the suitability of any family for family work, and could advise which group would best take them on.

As long as they were appropriate, referrals were accepted from any source – the duty workers, other area teams or outside agencies. Of course, this 'madness' required a method. In the steering group the alternatives were constantly reviewed and a detailed referral system continuously worked out and revised according to changing conditions. Just to assure readers that it is quite possible to organize a referral system across social work patch teams, here is one version tried and tested in our practice. It enabled the co-ordination of referrals from two area offices which occupied the same building and joined forces in the family workshop groups.

Let us look at the chart in *Figure* 7: the process begins at the far left corner (box 1). The duty social worker (or it may be any other worker in the office) asks herself, 'is this a family work referral?' after seeing a family member while on duty or receiving a referral from an external agency. We have trained all workers in the office to make appropriate judgements of this type. If the referral is not a family work one, the process is as usual in the office and is not included in this chart. Alternatively, the worker may feel that this is a family work referral or that she is 'not sure'. If she is not sure she can consult one of the family workshop leaders (box 2) who let their whereabouts be known to their administrative assistant. If she is sure, she has to judge how urgent the case is (box 3). If it can wait for two or three weeks she will channel it through the general family workshop referral book marking the name of the family, their address, the referral source, and the location of the family file if one already exists (box 4). If the case cannot wait she will try the Thursday afternoon slot book to see if there is a vacancy (box 5). She acts as in box 6 if a vacancy exists. If there is no vacancy there are clear instructions for alternative actions. It is important to prevent cases from falling between two stools. Therefore the instructions cover what to do with cases that are not taken up by the family workshop: either because there is no vacancy (box 10), or because further assessment (box 7) resulted in de-allocation of the case (box 9). The 'happy end' is, of course, at box 8 where allocation to family workshop is made.

We end this chapter here, but not before introducing a sobering thought. The structure presented may seem quite sophisticated and elaborate, and perhaps beyond your particular organization. If you feel this remember that we have presented you with abstract schemes. Day-to-day realities are far messier. Also, we should say that these are the products of a service that gradually developed over several years. The beginning was much simpler, smaller, and more modest. All we have tried to do is to share with you some of the lessons we have learned along the way. Your path may well be different, if only because you will work in somewhat different circumstances.

14 / WIDER
IMPLICATIONS

We have tried in this book to show how systemic thinking can be applied to work with families in a Social Services Department. Essentially, system theory offers a way of organizing our perceptions of phenomena at many different levels rather than seeing each in isolation from the other. It also provides an operational framework with which to approach different behaviours in the system. Any social worker who ventures to take a systemic approach to working with families will find it involves changes in her way of looking at the family and in understanding what is going on; she will also intervene in the family differently.

As indicated in previous chapters, the changes will involve quite specific skills – observational as well as those concerned with intervention. In Chapter 3 we suggested that the worker needs to develop an awareness of the non-verbal communication between family members. She needs to be able to see not only that mum frowns when offering tea, but also that dad clenches a fist at the same time. She needs to monitor which of these patterns tend to be repeated in the family, by whom, and in what order. It is these sequences, and their relation to verbal behaviours, that give the worker clues not only about the family's distress, but also (and equally important) about how maintaining the problem helps the family to preserve its steady state. The positive value of the problem to the family is a central systemic concept which the worker needs to acquire.

Certain basic interviewing skills are required in this work. Some are relatively easily derived from training in group work (because the family is a group), but others are specifically systemic (Palazzoli et al. 1980). In this book we stress the helpfulness of learning to be specific, to describe behaviours rather than ascribe feelings, to speak directly to the person concerned, etc. These all relate to effective interpersonal communication. The worker also needs to be able to teach these skills to the family so that they can learn to relate to each other more clearly and be more supportive. As experience grows through practice and training the worker learns to help restructure the family through 'the gentle art of reframing', the use of growth games, role-play, and the design of analogies. When appropriate, behavioural skills become an additional tool in her armoury.

However, the change to systemic thinking may have wider implications too. In Chapter 2 we offer a short statement of system theory as applied to family therapy, and suggest it is of key importance that the purpose of the work is to bring about a change in the family system of interaction before changes in the behaviour of individuals can take place. For the worker this involves a different relationship with the family; on the one hand, she uses more of herself and directs work quite openly; on the other, she takes care to stay out of the systemic 'game'. While being quite active, she also maintains emotional distance and is clearly selective with regard to the choice of the areas in which she is involved. There is an explicit understanding and agreement with the family about the work to be done and a shared responsibility for carrying it through. This means a more active/directive role for the worker who leads the process of change with the aim of helping the family quickly to take charge of it themselves. There is a strong emphasis on working with the positives, the strengths of the family. This usually implies a shift from long-term, open-ended involvement to a time-limited one, accompanied by far greater faith in the family's own capacity to solve problems and heal itself without the worker's direct intervention.

One of the positive aspects of the systemic approach is that no method is excluded; there is room for psychodynamic understanding, for the behavioural approach, and for action techniques. They can all be seen as various types of feedback that the worker offers the family. In Chapter 2 we indicate that there are three such mechanisms in the family system:

1 'Negative feedback' used to restore balance in the patterns of behaviour that have been disturbed.
2 'Positive feedback' employed to intensify some behaviours towards a more comprehensive change in the system.
3 'Meta feedback' which serves to charge behaviours with meaning and formulate the rules governing the system.

From a systemic point of view, the worker who forms 'a therapeutic system' with the family inevitably employs at least one of the three feedback mechanisms. It remains for future system analysts to begin to classify workers' interventions according to which mechanisms they employ. When this vast research project is achieved, it will be possible to indicate with more certainty what type of feedback may help at each point of the work and at each level of interaction.

When we are able to vary the type of our intervention systemically, it should become clear that one of the crucial skills for systemic work is the creation of analogies. The trained system analogist will be able to go up and down the ladder, from the minute detail of the internal experiences of the individual through intimate exchanges between couples to the transactions in families, groups, networks, and organizations, all the time remaining within system theory and employing one or more of the above three feedback mechanisms. Such a worker will be able to design analogy upon analogy like the layer upon layer of a well shaped onion. There are, of course, many types of analogies; they may be offered through modelling as in behaviour rehearsal (Bandura 1971; Lazarus 1966), through enactment as done in a whole range of growth games (Satir 1972), or through tasks and particularly paradoxical injunctions (Haley 1976; Hoffman 1981: 256–83). In Chapter 8 we discuss the use of symbolic analogies during the warm-up phase; the ability to listen to the family at all the levels simultaneously and draw out from this information images and metaphors that create space for family members to explore painful issues safely. In Chapter 9 we stress the importance of structural analogies. These seem particularly relevant to the practice of social work, since they enable the worker to cope with demands put on her from different directions. Although initially developed for in-session work (Minuchin 1974: Chapter 8), they can be extended to incorporate any source of influence outside the family, be it school, hospital, or a circle of friends. What matters is that the worker has the skill to act on the enlarged system as an analogy of the initial smaller one. For example, if the point is to get father more involved, this can happen at home (initial system) over the family meal, but equally so at school (enlarged system) when he discusses his daughter's achievements with the head teacher. All that matters is the worker's ability to pursue the structural change effort into the new context. She needs to identify and encourage the behaviour that is the equivalent of the change desired in the initial system (father's involvement in the above example).

As we learn to use analogies more widely we may come to accept that system theory can be applied to any level of human interaction. System theory may therefore prove a particularly useful conceptual framework for social workers who need to move continuously between the macro and micro levels. Although pretty ambitious, such a state of the art may not be as remote as it sometimes appears. It is encouraging to see systemic studies emerging at almost every level. Practitioners are beginning to work with the individual within this framework (Anchin and Kiesler 1982), suggesting that in fact there is no reason why we should not look at various internal experiences of the individual as sub-systems of the person as a whole. Systemic work with couples is well documented by now as part of the work with the family (Hoffman 1981). The thrust seems to extend also to groups where a comprehensive application of general system theory is now available (Durkin 1981) and in perhaps a somewhat looser way, also to networks (Maguire 1980) and organizations (Miller 1976; Schein 1969; Payne 1982). These are important developments that may help a great deal in the development of a comprehensive theory for social work. If appropriately incorporated they may fill some gaps and put flesh on the already accepted framework of the 'unitary approach' (Pincus and Minahan 1973; Goldstein 1973; Specht and Vickery 1977).

Obviously, this is still a long way ahead, but we would like to illustrate the potential usefulness of such a development in a final example from one of the most complex tasks of social work; that of adoption and fostering.

The transformation of a family into a network

The placement of a child in a permanent or temporary substitute family is already recognized as a central and complex task in social work by the creation of Adoption and Fostering Units in many local authority social services departments. Adoption and fostering is an example where all the levels previously mentioned interact. However, in spite of knowing that the adopted or fostered child is placed in a situation rather different from the natural nuclear family (Hazel 1981) many act as if their task was to 'normalize' the child; make the child feel as if nothing has radically changed. The intention behind this is undoubtedly noble. The child does need love and stability. It is just that with so many different carers around, any child is almost bound to feel confused and is very likely to act in confusing ways.

By the time a child is considered for adoption or fostering his parents must have suffered a great deal and he must have felt let down by them. A field social worker is involved, and often another worker at a residential setting if residential care has been necessary. The child's school may have taken some action and an EWO seen both parents and child. The natural parents might have sought treatment for drug addiction, for example, and a psychiatrist tried to help them. These 'multiple interventions' are necessary, yet too often each agent is acting in isolation from the others and tends to play the 'my child' game. Each may develop attachment to the child and feel she understands him best. Each is amazed that the others do not do more for this child. Such an approach seems to assume that it is best to 'normalize' the child by substituting the original bond he should have had with his parents with the new bond between him and the worker. When it comes to the stage of adoption or fostering the same ethos seems to be held by the prospective new 'parents'. How many primary bonds one child can develop is a question often left unanswered. No wonder the child begins to react in many strange and confusing ways while the adults around him are lost as to who is responsible for meeting his different needs.

We would like to suggest that the situation may be clarified and probably made easier if system theory is not only understood by those involved, but really assimilated and used in daily life.

We cannot, offer here either a full systemic analysis of adoption and fostering, or a comprehensive description of the skills involved. Space does not allow this and there is still a great deal unknown in the field. However, let us look at the situation again in very general terms, and from a system theory viewpoint. The child is initially part of the natural family system. We assume that the natural system has run into difficulties. These might have been presented through the child's behaviour or through that of the parents themselves. If the child presented the difficulties, the initial systemic response would be to attempt to help the natural system overcome the problem by working with the family as a whole. If the intervention in the natural system fails, the parents or some other agent may request fostering, adoption, or the reception into care of the child. Let us take the reception into care as an example.

However initiated, the move to receive a child into care amounts to the expansion of the family boundaries into the residential setting. Such an expansion can, at times, be helpful in that it gives the parents a breathing space to improve the situation; they may succeed in creating a different natural system into which they can later receive the child back. In such cases, the reception of a child into care can be short term and does not necessarily amount to separating the child from his natural system permanently. The residential worker has to supplement the missing natural parenting for a while and thus restore a certain balance in the child's system. We may say that the residential worker offers the natural family system 'negative feedback'; an intervention that creates stability in the whole system (the family) so that one part of it (the parents) can move towards change. The residential worker should appreciate the purpose of her involvement and keep the natural family system in mind as she helps the child go through this transitional period. For example, supportive links with the parents are important. If they are not maintained the child may not be ready to absorb the change that his parents have made in his absence and the return home may become a problem in itself.

If, on the other hand, the parents do not make changes that they or some other agent consider sufficient to enable the child to return home, something systemically different begins to happen. Whether prompted by the parents' initiative or that of a social worker, consideration of the child for adoption or fostering offers a different kind of feedback to the natural system. From saying that the natural system has a difficulty handling the child within its boundaries, events have moved to saying that it cannot contain the child at all. This is an intensification of the original difficulty, amplifying it to the point of involving a permanent extension of the natural system into another – the adoption or fostering one. Systemically, this can be seen as a 'positive feedback'. The difference is far from being semantic. With the introduction of positive feedback far more comprehensive changes are set in motion. Once positive feedback mechanisms operate, it is appropriate to expect second order change. The child will not only live with different people in a different place, but will enter a different set of rules where the meaning of events and social roles will be new. We refer to 'meta feedback' when the meaning of events and the rules governing them change. Of course, change happens all the time, but with second order change the infrastructure of the system shifts gear. The adopting or fostering 'family' cannot be expected to be in any way a replica of the child's natural family. A web of interrelationships among the substitute parents and a host of other sub-systems are set up around it. However 'good' the substitute parents, they will still need to remember and deal with the child's memories and feelings about his natural parents; they will have to liaise with a social worker and other agencies who may have to be involved, etc. It seems more appropriate to regard the new unit as a network with a number of sub-systems rather than hope for a 'normalization' of the child into a system that bears the semblance of a natural family but by definition cannot be one. This becomes more obvious from a system theory viewpoint. If consideration of adoption or fostering is a form of positive feedback then comprehensive second order change is set in motion and this is followed by meta feedback which charges the same behaviour (parenting) with new meanings (adopting or fostering) and inevitably generates new social roles and rules. The natural *family* system will thus be transformed into an adopting or fostering *network*.

It seems important to understand this for two reasons: first, if everybody accepted that the natural family situation cannot be replicated in adoption or fostering, it would be easier to negotiate the new respective roles into which substitute parents, social workers, and others have to enter in the emerging network. Fewer people would need to play the over-protective 'my child' game; more of them would be able to co-operate with each other more easily. The second reason has to do with fact that the response to positive feedback is unpredictable. If the initiative for adoption or fostering has come from the social worker, the natural parents may contest it in court. This, it should be remembered, may not be a bad thing. For the natural parents to win the case in court, they need to present evidence that they are now willing and able to look after the child themselves. If we look at the situation systemically we see that in this scenario the social worker makes positive feedback by planning for adoption or fostering. The natural parents will have to respond with making considerable changes in their lives in order to oppose this. They will have to introduce positive feedback into their own system. Indeed, that is what the social worker hoped for in the first place. Sometimes positive feedback from one system can evoke the same from another. Social workers can be helped by understanding this, so that when the natural parents oppose their move, they are ready to consider the possibility that the parents have now responded to their initiative and have introduced the desired change rather than simply 'feigning' changing with the help of a good lawyer.

This brief illustrative discussion suggests that system theory can help us anticipate some of the general features of some highly complex situations. It also alerts us to the need to work and intervene at different levels of interaction; continuously to create analogies – from the micro level of the internal experiences of the child through the marital relationship of his natural parents, to family interactions, to the relationships between families and the Social Services Department, and further on, to the interactions among the host of agencies that are drawn into the situation. Finally, we reach a state of affairs where skills of negotiating network relationships are crucial. We believe that many of the specific skills mentioned in this book are very relevant to facilitating various stages in this process.

If system theory is further developed and tested in practice, we may one day be freed from the need either to choose the best method or to rely solely on our intuition in our work (Byng-Hall and Campbell 1981). Instead, we shall be able to mix and combine all the interventions that have proved useful, conceiving them as forms of feedback we can make into an identified system of interactions. Planning our interventions will then be a matter of considering a number of elements in their relations to each other, with at least four questions in mind:

1 What type of *feedback* to make?
2 Into what *part of the system*?
3 At what *level*?
4 At what *stage* of the work?

Finding detailed replies may well be one of the more exciting ventures in the future and we hope many practitioners and scholars will collaborate in providing them.

APPENDIX I
A BASIC
READING LIST

THE FAMILY LIFE CYCLE

Carter, E. A. and McGoldrick, M. (eds) (1980) *The Family Life Cycle*. New York: Gardner Press.

INTRODUCTORY TEXTBOOKS TO FAMILY THERAPY

Andolfi, M. (1979) *Family Therapy: An Interactional Approach*. New York: Plenum Press.
Walrond-Skinner, S. (1976) *Family Therapy: The Treatment of Natural Systems*. London: Routledge & Kegan Paul.
Hoffman, L. (1981) *Foundations of Family Therapy*. New York: Basic Books.

DIFFERENT FAMILY THERAPY STYLES

The communication style
Satir, V. (1967) *Conjoint Family Therapy*. Palo Alto, Calif.: Science & Behavior Books.
Satir, V. (1972) *Peoplemaking*. Palo Alto, Calif.: Science & Behavior Books.

The structural style
Minuchin, S. (1974) *Families and Family Therapy*. London: Tavistock Publications.

The strategic style
Haley, J. (1976) *Problem Solving Therapy*. London: Jossey-Bass.
Palazzoli, M. S., Cecchin, G., Prata, G., and Boscolo, L. (1978) *Paradox and Counterparadox*. London: Jason Aronson.

The behavioural style
Patterson, G. R. (1971) *Families*. Champaign, Illinois: Research Press.
Peine, H. and Howarth, R. (1975) *Children and Parents: Everyday Problems of Behaviour*. Harmondsworth: Penguin.

The psychodynamic style
Ackerman, N. W. (1966) *Treating the Troubled Family*. New York: Basic Books.
Bowen, M. (1978) *Family Therapy in Clinical Practice*. New York: Jason Aronson.

The network style
Reuveni, R. (1979) *Networking Families in Crisis*. London: Human Science Press.

APPENDIX II
CONTRIBUTIONS TO
THIS HANDBOOK

As mentioned in the preface, various chapters in this handbook are the prime contribution of different members of the group, each benefiting from comments and suggestions from all the others. The individual contributions are as follows:

Part I

Chapter 1	A guide to this handbook	by Oded Manor
Chapter 2	Theory before practice	by Denise Mumford
Chapter 3	A period of preparation	by Denise Mumford

Part II

An outline of events		by Denise Mumford
Chapter 4	Phases of family work	by Oded Manor
Chapter 5	The referral phase	by Denise Mumford
Chapter 6	Clearing the field	by Oded Manor
Chapter 7	Induction	by Bridget Walker
Chapter 8	Warming up	by Jeanne Bertrand and Bridget Walker
Chapter 9	Approaching the crucial focus	by Oded Manor
Chapter 10	Consolidating change	by Bridget Walker
Chapter 11	Maintenance and the closure of cases	by Oded Manor and Denise Mumford

REFERENCES

Abrams, P. (1980) Social Change, Social Networks and Neighbourhood Care. *Social Work Service* **22**: 12–23.

Ackerman, N. W. (1966) *Treating the Troubled Family*. New York: Basic Books.

Adams, J., Hayes, J., and Hopson, B. (1976) *Transition: Understanding and Managing Personal Change*. London: Martin Robertson.

Adams, R. (1980) Naming of Parts: Support Groups for Family Therapy Practice. *Social Work Service* **22**: 24–8.

Addison, C. (1982) A Defence against the Public? Aspects of Intake in Social Services Departments. *British Journal of Social Work* **12**(6): 605–18.

Anchin, J. C. and Kiesler, D. J. (eds) (1982) *Handbook of Interpersonal Psychotherapy*. New York: Pergamon Press.

Andolfi, M. (1979) *Family Therapy: An Interactional Approach*. New York: Plenum Press.

Bandura, A. (1971) *Social Learning Theory*. Morristown, New Jersey: General Learning Press.

Bayley, M. (1981) Neighbourhood Care and Community Care: A Response to Philip Abrams. *Social Work Service* **26**: 4–9.

Becvar, R. J. (1974) *Skills for Effective Communication*. Chichester: John Wiley.

Beels, C. C. (1969) Family Therapy: A View. *Family Process* **8**(2): 290–99.

Behrens, M. L., Meyers, D. I., Goldfarb B., Goldfarb, N., and Fieldsteel, N. D. (1969) The Henry Ittelson Centre Family Interaction Scales. *Genetic Psychology Monographs* **80**(1): 205–95.

Bentovim, A. (1979) Towards Creating a Focal Hypothesis for Brief Focal Family Therapy. *Journal of Family Therapy* **1**(2): 125–36.

Bertalanffy, L. von (1968) *General System Theory: Foundations, Development, Applications*. New York: Braziller.

Blatner, H. (1973) *Acting In: Practical Applications of Psychodramatic Methods*. New York: Springer.

Bowen, M. (1978) *Family Therapy in Clinical Practice*. New York: Jason Aronson.

Byng-Hall, J. and Campbell, D. (1981) Resolving Conflicts in Family Distance Regulation: An Integrative Approach. *Journal of Marital and Family Therapy* 7: 321–30.

Bywaters, P. (1975a) Ending Casework Relationships (1). *Social Work Today* 6(10): 301–04.

———— (1975b) Ending Casework Relationships (2). *Social Work Today* 6(11): 336–38.

Carpenter, J., Treacher, A., Jenkins, H., and O'Reilly, P. (1982) Oh, no! Not the Smiths Again, Part II. *Journal of Family Therapy* 4(4): 81–96.

Carter, E. A. and McGoldrick, M. (eds) (1980) *The Family Life Cycle*. New York: Gardner Press.

Combrinck-Graham, L. (1980) Termination in Family Therapy. In A. S. Gurman (ed) *Questions and Answers in the Practice of Family Therapy*. New York: Brunner/Mazel.

Cornwell, M. and Pearson, R. (1981) Co-therapy Teams and One-Way Screens in Family Therapy Practice and Research. *Family Process* 20(2): 199–210.

Corsini, R. J. (1966) *Role Playing in Psychotherapy*. Chicago: Aldine.

Daniell, D. (1981) Transitions in the Family Life Cycle. Paper presented at the Tavistock Institute of Human Relations, Social Work Continuation Group, 14 November.

Dell, P. S. (1982) Beyond Homeostasis: Towards a Concept of Coherence. *Family Process* 21: 21–41.

Duhl, F. J., Kantor, D., and Duhl, B. S. (1973) Learning, Space and Action in Family Therapy: A Primer in Sculpture. In D. A. Bloch (ed) *Techniques of Family Psychotherapy*. New York: Grune & Stratton.

Durkin, J. E. (ed) (1981) *Living Groups; Group Psychotherapy and General System Theory*. New York: Brunner/Mazel.

Egan, G. (1975) *The Skilled Helper*. Monterey, Calif.: Brooks/Cole.

Ezriel, H. (1950) A Psychoanalytic Approach to Group Treatment. *British Journal Medical Psychology* 23: 59–74.

Goldstein, A. P. and Kanfer, F. H. (eds) (1979) *Maximizing Treatment Gains*. London: Academic Press.

Goldstein, H. (1973) *Social Work Practice: A Unitary Approach*. Columbia, S. Carolina: University of S. Carolina Press.

Gordon, D. (1978) *Therapeutic Metaphors*. Cupertino, Calif.: Meta Press.

Hadley, R. and McGrath, M. (1980) *Going Local*. NCVO Occasional Paper 1. London: Bedford Square Press.

Haley, J. (1963) *Strategies of Psychotherapy*. New York: Grune & Stratton.

———— (1976) *Problem Solving Therapy*. London: Jossey-Bass.

Haley, J. and Hoffman, L. (1967) *Techniques of Family Therapy*. New York: Basic Books.

Hannum, J. W. (1980) Some Co-therapy Techniques with Families. *Family Process* **19**(2): 161–68.

Hartman, L. A. (1979) The Extended Family as a Resource for Change. In C. B. Germain (ed) *Social Work Practice*. New York: Columbia University Press.

Hazel, N. (1981) *A Bridge to Independence*. Oxford: Basil Blackwell.

Hoffman, L. (1981) *Foundations of Family Therapy*. New York: Basic Books.

Hurley, J. and Manor, O. (1977) The Family Workshop Two Years On, Unpublished paper. London Borough of Wandsworth Social Services.

Hutton, J. M. (1977) *Short-Term Contracts in Social Work*. London: Routledge & Kegan Paul.

Iveson, C., Sharps, P., and Whiffen, R. (1971) A Family Therapy Workshop: A Review of a Two-Year Experiment in a Social Services Department. *Journal of Family Therapy* **1**: 397–408.

Jenkins, J., Hildrebrand, J., and Lask, B. (1982) Failure: An Exploration and Survival Kit. *Journal of Family Therapy* **4**(3): 307–20.

Kantor, D. and Lehr, W. (1975) *Inside the Family*. London: Jossey-Bass.

Keith, D. V. and Whitaker, C. A. (1977) The Divorce Labyrinth. In P. Papp (ed) *Family Therapy: Full Length Case Studies*. New York: Gardner Press.

Laing, R. D. (1970) *Knots*. London: Tavistock Publications.

Lazarus, A. A. (1966) Behavior Rehearsal vs. Non-Directive Therapy vs. Advice in Effecting Behavior Change. *Behavior Research and Therapy* **4**: 209–12.

Lidz, T. (1974) *Family and Marital Therapy*. New York: Grune & Stratton.

Lieberman, S. (1982) Going Back to Your Own Family. In A. Bentovim, G. Gorell-Barnes, and A. Cooklin (eds) *Family Therapy*, vol. 1. London: Academic Press.

McGoldrick, M., Pearce, J. K., and Giordiano, J. (eds) (1982) *Ethnicity and Family Therapy*. London: The Guildford Press.

Maguire, L. (1980) The Interface of Social Workers with Personal Networks. *Social Work with Groups* **3**(3): 39–49.

Mann, J. (1973) *Time-Limited Psychotherapy*. Cambridge, Mass.: Harvard University Press.

Mattison, J. (1977) *The Reflection Process in Casework Supervision*. London: Institute of Marital Studies, Tavistock Institute of Human Relations.

Menzies, I. E. P. (1970) The Functioning of Social Systems as a Defence against Anxiety. London: Centre for Applied Social Research, Tavistock Institute of Human Relations.

Miller, E. (ed) (1976) *Task and Organisation*. New York: John Wiley & Sons.

Minuchin, S. (1974) *Families and Family Therapy*. London: Tavistock Publications.

Minuchin, S. and Fishman, H. C. (1981) *Family Therapy Techniques*. Cambridge, Mass.: Harvard University Press.

Olson, D. H., Sprenkle, D. H., and Russel, C. S. (1979) Circumplex Model of Marital and Family Systems: I. *Family Process* **18**(1): 3–27.

Open University (1980) *Conflict in the Family*. Milton Keynes: Open University Press.

Orbach, S. (1978) *Fat is a Feminist Issue*. London: Paddington Press.

Palazzoli, M. S., Boscolo, L., Cecchin, G. and Prata, G., (1980) Hypothesising–Circularity –Neutrality: Three Guidelines for the Conductor of the Session. *Family Process* **19**(1): 3–12.

Palazzoli, M. S., Cecchin, G., Prata, G., and Boscolo, L. (1978) *Paradox and Counterparadox*. London: Jason Aronson.

Papp, P., Silverstein, O., and Carter, E. (1973) Family Sculpture in Prevention Work with 'Well Families'. *Family Process* **12**: 197–212.

Patterson, G. R. (1971) *Families*. Champaign, Illinois: Research Press.

Payne, M. (1982) *Working in Teams*. London: British Association of Social Work Publications, The McMillan Press.

Peine, H. and Howarth, R. (1975) *Children and Parents: Everyday Problems of Behaviour*. Harmondsworth: Penguin.

Pincus, A. and Minahan, A. (1973) *Social Work Practice*. Itasca, Illinois: F. E. Peacock.

Pincus, L. and Dare, C. (1978) *Secrets in the Family*. London: Faber & Faber.

Reuveni, R. (1979) *Networking Families in Crisis*. London: Human Science Press.

Rowbottom, R., Hey, A., and Billis, D. (1974) *Social Services Departments*. London: Heinemann.

Satir, V. (1967) *Conjoint Family Therapy*. Palo Alto, Calif.: Science & Behavior Books.

———— (1972) *Peoplemaking*. Palo Alto, Calif.: Science & Behavior Books.

Schein, E. H. (1969) *Process Consultation: Its Role in Organisation Development*. London: Addison-Wesley.

Seabury, B. A. (1976) The Contract: Uses, Abuses and Limitations. *Social Work* (New York) **21**(1): 16–21.

Skynner, A. C. R. (1971) The Minimum Sufficient Network. *Social Work Today* **2**(9): 3–7.

———— (1976) *One Flesh, Separate Persons*. London: Constable.

Small, L. (1979) *The Briefer Psychotherapies*, revised edition. New York: Brunner/ Mazel.

Smith, M. (1965) *Professional Education for Social Work in Britain: A Historical Account*. London: George Allen & Unwin.

Specht, H. and Vickery, A. (1977) *Integrating Social Work Methods*. London: George Allen & Unwin.

Speck, R. V. and Attneave, C. L. (1973) *Family Networks*. New York: Vintage Books.

Stierlin, H., Rucker-Embden, I., Wetzel, N., and Wirsching, M. (1980) *The First Interview with the Family*. New York: Brunner/Mazel.

Swenson, C. (1979) Social Networks, Mutual Aid and the Life Model of Practice. In C. B. Germain (ed) *Social Work Practice*. New York: Columbia University Press.

Teismann, M. (1980) Convening Strategies in Family Therapy. *Family Process* **19**: 393–400.

Terkelsen, A. G. (1980) Towards a Theory of the Family Life Cycle. In A. E. Carter and M. McGoldrick (eds) *The Family Life Cycle*. New York: Gardner Press.

Treacher, A. and Carpenter, J. (1982) Oh no! Not the Smiths Again! Part I. *Journal of Family Therapy* **4**(3): 285–305.

Walrond-Skinner, S. (1976) *Family Therapy*. London: Routledge & Kegan Paul.

Walsh, F. (ed) (1982) *Normal Family Processes*. London: The Guildford Press.

Watzlawick, P., Beavin, J. H., and Jackson, D. D. (1967) *Pragmatics of Human Communication*. New York: W. W. Norton & Co.

Watzlawick, P., Weakland, J., and Fisch, R. (1974) *Change*. New York: W. W. Norton & Co.

Weakland, J. H., Fisch, R., Watzlawick, P., and Bodin, A. M. (1974) Brief Therapy: Focused Problem Resolution. *Family Process* **13**(2): 141–68.

Whiffen, R. and Byng-Hall, J. (eds) (1982) *Family Therapy Supervision*. London: Academic Press.

INDEX